Puffin Classics

WHAT KATY DID
AT SCHOOL

'These home cares are making you old before your time.
It will do you and Clover both good, and once you are
settled at Hillsover, you'll be very happy, I hope.'

As Katy and her sister near their forbidding destina-
tion, being happy is not exactly what they anticipate,
with thirty-two school rules nailed up on all the doors
and the prospect of tight-lipped Mrs Nipson on the
prowl. But at least the girls can share a room together in
Quaker Row – and Rose Red is right next door!

Katy and Clover are determined to make the best of
things, and soon discover that school days are by no
means always smooth and can be an awful lot of fun!

Born in Cleveland, Ohio, in 1835, Susan Coolidge
wrote three books about Katy Carr. The first, *What Katy
Did,* was published in 1872, followed a year later by
What Katy Did at School and by *What Katy Did Next* in
1886. All three books are published in Puffin Classics,
complete and unabridged.

Susan Coolidge

WHAT KATY DID AT SCHOOL

PUFFIN BOOKS

Puffin Books, Penguin Books Ltd, Harmondsworth, Middlesex, England
Viking Penguin Inc., 40 West 23rd Street, New York, New York 10010, U.S.A.
Penguin Books Australia Ltd, Ringwood, Victoria, Australia
Penguin Books Canada Ltd, 2801 John Street, Markham, Ontario, Canada L3R 1B4
Penguin Books (N.Z.) Ltd, 182–190 Wairau Road, Auckland 10, New Zealand

First published 1873
Published in Puffin Books 1985
Reprinted 1985

Printed and bound in Great Britain by
Cox & Wyman Ltd, Reading
Set in Linotron Palatino
by Rowland Phototypesetting Ltd,
Bury St Edmunds, Suffolk

CONTENTS

1   Conic Section   7

2   A New Year and a New Plan   24

3   On the Way   37

4   The Nunnery   49

5   Roses and Thorns   62

6   The S.S.U.C.   75

7   Injustice   94

8   Changes   107

9   The Autumn Vacation   120

10 A Budget of Letters   141

11 Christmas Boxes   155

12 Waiting for Spring   171

13 Paradise Regained   181

CHAPTER
1

CONIC SECTION

It was just after that happy visit mentioned at the end of 'What Katy Did', that Elsie and John made their famous excursion to Conic Section – an excursion which neither of them ever forgot, and about which the family teased them for a long time afterwards.

The summer had been cool; but, as often happens after cool summers, the autumn proved unusually hot. It seemed as if the months had been playing a game, and had 'changed places' all round; and as if September were determined to show that he knew how to make himself just as disagreeable as August, if only he chose to do so.

All the last half of Cousin Helen's stay the weather was excessively sultry. She felt it very much, though the children did all they could to make her comfortable, with shaded rooms, and iced water, and fans. Every evening the boys would wheel her sofa out on the porch, in hopes of coolness; but it was of no use: the evenings were as warm as the days, and the yellow dust hanging in the air made the sunshine look thick and hot. A few bright leaves appeared on the trees, but they were wrinkled, and of an ugly colour. Clover said she thought they had been *boiled* red like lobsters. Altogether, the month was a trying one, and the coming of October made little or no difference; still the dust continued, and the heat; and the wind, when it blew, had no refreshment in it, but seemed to have passed over some great furnace, which had burned out of it all life and flavour.

In spite of this, however, it was wonderful to see how Katy gained and improved. Every day added to her powers. First she came down to dinner, then to breakfast. She sat on the porch in the afternoons; she poured the tea. It was like a miracle to the others, in the beginning, to watch her going about the house; but they got used to it surprisingly soon – one does to pleasant things. One person, however, never got used to it, never took it as a matter of course; and that was Katy herself. She could not run downstairs, or out into the garden; she could not open the kitchen door to give an order, without a sense of gladness and exultation which was beyond words. The wider and more active life stimulated her in every way. Her cheeks grew round and pink, her eyes bright. Cousin Helen and papa watched this change with indescribable pleasure; and Mrs Worrett, who dropped in to lunch one day, fairly screamed with surprise at the sight of it.

'To think of it!' she cried, 'why, the last time I was here you looked as if you had taken root in that chair of yours for the rest of your days, and here you are stepping around as lively as I be! Well, well! wonders will never cease. It does my eyes good to see you, Katherine. I wish your poor aunt were here today; that I do. How pleased she'd be!'

It is doubtful whether Aunt Izzie would have been so pleased, for the lived-in look of the best parlour would have horrified her extremely; but Katy did not recollect that just then. She was touched at the genuine kindness of Mrs Worrett's voice, and took very willingly her offered kiss. Clover brought lemonade and grapes, and they all devoted themselves to making the poor lady comfortable. Just before she went away, she said:

'How is it that I can't never get any of you to come out to Conic Section? I'm sure I've asked you often enough. There's Elsie, now, and John; they're just the age to enjoy being in the country. Why won't you send 'em out for a week? Johnnie can feed chickens, and chase 'em too, if she likes,' she added, as Johnnie dashed then into view, pursuing one of Phil's bantams round the house. 'Tell her so, won't you, Katherine? There is lots of chickens on the farm. She can chase 'em from morning to night, if she's a mind to.'

Katy thanked her, but she didn't think the children would care to go. She gave Johnnie the message, and then the whole matter passed out of her mind. She was surprised, a few days later, by having it brought up again by Elsie. The family were in low spirits that morning because of Cousin Helen's having just gone away; and Elsie was lying on the sofa, fanning herself with a great palm-leaf fan.

'Oh, dear!' she sighed. 'Do you suppose it's ever going to be cool again in this world? It does seem as if I couldn't bear it any longer.'

'Aren't you well, darling?' inquired Katy, anxiously.

'Oh, yes! well enough,' replied Elsie. 'It's only this horrid heat, and never going away to where it's cooler. I keep thinking about the country, and wishing I was there feeling the wind blow. I wonder if papa wouldn't let John and me go to Conic Section and see Mrs Worrett. Do you think he would if you asked him?'

'But,' said Katy, amazed, 'Conic Section isn't exactly country, you know. It is just out of the city – only six miles from here. And Mrs Worrett's house is close to the road, papa said. Do you think you'd like it, dear? It *can't* be very much cooler than this.'

'Oh, yes! it can,' rejoined Elsie, in a tone which was a little fretful. 'It's quite near woods; Mrs Worrett told me so. Besides, it's *always* cooler on a farm. There's more room for the wind, and – oh, everything's pleasanter! You can't think how tired I am of this hot house. Last night I hardly slept at all; and, when I did, I dreamed that I was a loaf of brown bread, and Debby was putting me into the oven to bake. It was a horrid dream. I was so glad to wake up. Won't you ask papa if we may go, Katy?'

'Why, of course I will, if you wish it so much. Only' – Katy stopped, and did not finish her sentence. A vision of fat Mrs Worrett had risen before her, and she could not help doubting if Elsie would find the farm as pleasant as she expected. But sometimes the truest kindness is in giving people their own unwise way, and Elsie's eyes looked so wistful that Katy had no heart to argue or refuse.

Dr Carr looked doubtful when the plan was proposed to him.

'It's too hot,' he said. 'I don't believe the girls will like it.'

'Oh, yes; we will, papa; indeed we will,' pleaded Elsie and John, who had lingered near the door to learn the fate of their request.

Dr Carr smiled at the imploring faces, but he looked a little quizzical. 'Very well,' he said, 'you may go. Mr Worrett is coming into town tomorrow on some bank business. I'll send word by him; and in the afternoon, when it is cooler, Alexander can drive you out.'

'Goody! Goody!' cried John, jumping up and down, while Elsie put her arms round papa's neck and gave him a hug.

'And Thursday I'll send for you,' he continued.

'But, papa,' expostulated Elsie, 'that's only two days. Mrs Worrett said a week.'

'Yes, she said a week,' chimed in John; 'and she's got ever so many chickens, and I'm to feed 'em, and chase 'em about as much as I like. Only it's too hot to run much,' she added reflectively.

'You won't really send for us on Thursday, will you, papa?' urged Elsie, anxiously. 'I'd like to stay ever and ever so long; but Mrs Worrett said a week.'

'I shall send on Thursday,' repeated Dr Carr in a decided tone. Then, seeing that Elsie's lip was trembling, and her eyes were full of tears, he continued: 'Don't look so woeful, Pussy. Alexander shall drive out for you; but if you want to stay longer, you may send him back with a note to say what day you would like to have him come again. Will that do?'

'Oh, yes!' said Elsie, wiping her eyes; 'that will do beautifully, papa. Only, it seems such a pity that Alexander should have to go twice when it's so hot; for we're sure to want to stay a week.'

Papa only laughed as he kissed her. All being settled, the children began to get ready. It was quite an excitement packing the bags, and deciding what to take and what not to take. Elsie grew bright and gay with the bustle. Just to think of being in the country – the cool, green country – made her perfectly happy, she declared. The truth was, she was a little feverish, and not quite well, and didn't know exactly how she felt or what she wanted.

The drive out was pleasant, except that Alexander upset John's gravity, and hurt Elsie's dignity very much, by inquiring, as they left the gate, 'Do the little misses know where it is that they want to go?' Part of the way the road ran through woods. They were rather boggy woods; but the dense shade kept off the sun, and there was a spicy smell of evergreens and sweet fern. Elsie felt that the good time had fairly begun, and her spirits rose with every turn of the wheels.

By and by they left the woods, and came out again into the sunshine. The road was dusty, and so were the fields, and the ragged sheaves of cornstalks which dotted them here and there looked dusty too. Piles of dusty-red apples lay on the grass, under the orchard trees. Some cows going down a lane toward their milking shed mooed in a dispirited and thirsty way, which made the children feel thirsty also.

'I want a drink of water very badly,' said John. 'Do you suppose it's much farther? How long will it be before we get to Mrs Worrett's, Alexander?'

''Most there, miss,' replied Alexander laconically.

Elsie put her head out of the carriage, and looked eagerly round. Where was the delightful farm? She saw a big, pumpkin-coloured house by the roadside, a little farther on; but surely that couldn't be it! Yes; Alexander drew up at the gate, and jumped down to lift them out. It really was! The surprise quite took away her breath.

She looked about. There were the woods, to be sure, but half a mile away across the fields. Near the house there were no trees at all; only some lilac bushes at one side; there was no green grass either. A gravel path took up the whole of the narrow front yard; and, what with the blazing colour of the paint, and the wide-awake look of the blindless windows, the house had somehow the air of standing on tiptoe and staring hard at something – the dust in the road, perhaps, for there seemed nothing else to stare at.

Elsie's heart sank indescribably, as she and John got very slowly out of the vehicle, and Alexander, putting his arm over the fence, rapped loudly at the front door. It was some minutes before the rap was answered. Then a heavy step was heard creaking through the hall, and somebody began fumbling at an obstinate bolt, which would not move. Next, a voice which they recognized as Mrs Worrett's, called, 'Isaphiny! Isaphiny! come and see if you can open this door.'

'How funny!' whispered Johnnie, beginning to giggle.

'Isaphiny' seemed to be upstairs, for presently they heard her running down, after which a fresh rattle began at the obstinate bolt. But still the door did not open, and at length Mrs Worrett put her lips to the keyhole, and asked –

'Who is it?'

The voice sounded so hollow and ghostly, that Elsie

jumped, as she answered: 'It's I, Mrs Worrett – Elsie Carr. And Johnnie's here, too.'

'Ts, ts, ts!' sounded from within, and then came a whispering, after which Mrs Worrett put her mouth again to the keyhole, and called out:

'Go round to the back, children. I can't make this door open anyway. It's all swelled up with the damp.'

'Damp!' whispered Johnnie, 'why, it hasn't rained since the third week in August; papa said so yesterday.'

'That's nothing, Miss Johnnie,' put in Alexander, over-hearing her. 'Folks here away don't open their front doors much – only for weddings, and funerals, and such like. Very likely this has stood shut these five years. I know the last time I drove Miss Carr out before she died, it was just so; and she had to go round to the back as you're a-doing now.'

John's eyes grew wide with wonder, but there was no time to say anything, for they had turned the corner of the house, and there was Mrs Worrett waiting at the kitchen door to receive them. She looked fatter than ever, Elsie thought; but she kissed them both, and said she was real glad to see a Carr in her house at last.

'It was too bad,' she went on, 'to keep you waiting so. But the fact is I got asleep, and when you knocked I waked up all in a daze, and for a minute it didn't come to me who it must be. Take the bags right upstairs, Isaphiny, and put them in the keeping-room chamber. How's your pa, Elsie – and Katy? Not laid up again, I hope.'

'Oh, no; she seems to get better all the time.'

'That's right,' responded Mrs Worrett, heartily. 'I didn't know, but what, with hot weather, and company in the house, and all – there's a chicken, Johnnie,' she exclaimed, suddenly interrupting herself, as a long-legged hen ran past the door. 'Want to chase it right away? You can if you like. Or would you rather go upstairs first?'

'Upstairs, please,' replied John, while Elsie went to the door, and watched Alexander driving away down the dusty road. She felt as if their last friend had deserted them. Then she and Johnnie followed Isaphiny upstairs. Mrs Worrett never 'mounted' in hot weather, she told them.

The spare chamber was just under the roof. It was very hot, and smelled as if the windows had never been opened since the house was built. As soon as they were alone, Elsie ran across the room and threw up the sash; but the moment she let go down it fell again, with a crash that shook the floor and made the pitcher dance and rattle in the washbowl. The children were dreadfully frightened, especially when they heard Mrs Worrett at the foot of the stairs calling to ask what was the matter.

'It's only the window,' explained Elsie, going into the hall. 'I'm so sorry, but it won't stay open. Something's the matter with it.'

'Did you stick the nail in?' inquired Mrs Worrett.

'The nail? No, ma'am.'

'Why, how on earth did you expect it to stay up, then? You young folks never see what's before your eyes. Look on the window-sill, and you'll find it. It's put there a-purpose.'

Elsie returned, much discomfited. She looked, and, sure enough, there was a big nail, and there was a hole in the side of the window-frame in which to stick it. This time she got the window open without accident; but a long blue paper shade caused her much embarrassment. It hung down, and kept the air from coming in. She saw no way of fastening it.

'Roll it up and put in a pin,' suggested John.

'I'm afraid of tearing the paper. Dear, what a horrid thing it is!' replied Elsie, in a disgusted tone.

However, she stuck in a couple of pins and fastened the shade out of the way. After that they looked about the room. It was plainly furnished, but very nice and neat. The bureau was covered with a white towel, on which stood a pincushion, with 'Remember Ruth' stuck upon it in pins. John admired this very much, and felt that she could never make up her mind to spoil the pattern by taking out a pin, however great her need of one might be.

'What a high bed!' she exclaimed. 'Elsie, you'll have to climb on a chair to get into it; and so shall I.'

Elsie felt it. 'Feathers!' she cried, in a tone of horror. 'O John! why did we come? What shall we do?'

'I guess we shan't mind it much,' replied John, who was perfectly well, and considered these little variations on home habits rather as fun than otherwise. But Elsie gave a groan. Two nights on a feather-bed! How should she bear it!

Tea was ready in the kitchen when they went down-stairs. A little fire had been lighted to boil the water. It was almost out, but the room felt stiflingly warm, and the butter was so nearly melted that Mrs Worrett had to help it with a teaspoon. Buzzing flies hovered above the table, and gathered thick on the plate of cake. The bread was excellent, and so were the cottage cheeses and the stewed quince; but Elsie could eat nothing. She was in a fever of heat. Mrs Worrett was distressed at this want of appetite, and so was Mr Worrett, to whom the children had just been introduced. He was a kindly-looking old man, with a bald head, who came to supper in his shirt sleeves, and was as thin as his wife was fat.

'I'm afraid the little girl don't like her supper, Lucinda,' he said. 'You must see about getting her something different tomorrow.'

'Oh! it isn't that. Everything is very nice, only I'm not hungry,' pleaded Elsie, feeling as if she should like to cry. She did cry a little after tea, as they sat in the dusk; Mr Worrett smoking his pipe and slapping mosquitoes outside the door, and Mrs Worrett sleeping rather noisily in a big rocking-chair. But not even Johnnie found out that she was crying, for Elsie felt that she was the naughtiest child in the world to behave so badly when everybody was so kind to her. She repeated this to herself many times, but it didn't do much good. As often as the thought of home and Katy and papa came, a wild longing to get back to them would rush over her, and her eyes would fill again with sudden tears.

The night was very uncomfortable. Not a breath of wind was stirring, or none found its way to the stifling bed where the little sisters lay. John slept pretty well, in spite of heat and mosquitoes, but Elsie hardly closed her eyes. Once she got up and went to the window, but the blue-paper shade had become unfastened, and rattled down upon her head with a sudden bump, which startled her very much. She could find no pins in the dark, so she left it hanging; whereupon it rustled and flapped through the rest of the night, and did its share toward keeping her awake. About three o'clock she fell into a doze; and it seemed only a minute after that before she woke up to find bright sunshine in the room, and half-a-dozen roosters crowing and calling under the windows. Her head ached violently. She longed to stay in bed, but feared Mrs Worrett would think it impolite: so she dressed and went down with Johnnie; but she looked so pale, and ate so little breakfast, that Mrs Worrett was quite troubled, and said she had better not try to go out, but just lie on the lounge in the best room, and amuse herself with a book.

The lounge in the best room was covered with slippery, purple chintz. It was a high lounge, and very narrow. There was nothing at the end to hold a pillow in its place; so the pillow constantly tumbled off and jerked Elsie's head suddenly backward, which was not at all comfortable. Worse, Elsie having dropped into a doze, she herself tumbled to the floor, rolling from the glassy, smooth chintz as if it had been a slope of ice. This adventure made her so nervous that she dared not go to sleep again, though Johnnie fetched two chairs, and placed them beside the sofa to hold her on. So she followed Mrs Worrett's advice, and 'amused herself with a book'. There were not many books in the best room. The one Elsie chose was a fat black volume called 'The Complete Works of Mrs Hannah More'. Part of it was prose, and part was poetry. Elsie began with a chapter called 'Hints on the Formation of the Character of a Youthful Princess'. But there were a great many long words in it; so she turned to a story named 'Coelebs in Search of a Wife'. It was about a young gentleman who wanted to get married, but who didn't feel sure that there were any young ladies nice enough for him; so he went about making visits, first to one and then to another; and, when he had stayed a few days at a house, he would always say, 'No, she won't do,' and then he would go away. At last he found a young lady who seemed the very person, who visited the poor, and got up early in the morning, and always wore white, and never forgot to wind up her watch or do her duty; and Elsie almost thought that now the difficult young gentleman must be satisfied, and say, 'This is the very thing.' When, lo! her attention wandered a little, and the next thing she knew she was rolling off the lounge for the second time, in company with Mrs Hannah More. They landed in the chairs, and Johnnie ran and picked them both up. Altogether, lying on the best parlour sofa was not very restful; and as the day went on, and the sun beating on the blindless windows made the room hotter, Elsie grew continually more and more feverish and home-sick and disconsolate.

Meanwhile Johnnie was kept in occupation by Mrs Worrett, who had got the idea firmly fixed in her mind that the chief joy in a child's life was to chase chickens. Whenever a hen fluttered past the kitchen door, which was about once in three minutes, she would cry, 'Here, Johnnie, here's another chicken for you to chase'; and poor Johnnie would feel obliged to dash out into the sun. Being a very polite little girl, she did not like to say to Mrs Worrett that running in the heat was disagreeable; so by dinner-time she was thoroughly tired out, and would have been cross if she had known how; but she didn't – Johnnie was never cross. After dinner it was even worse; for the sun was hotter, and the chickens, who didn't mind sun, seemed to be walking all the time. 'Hurry, Johnnie, here's another!' came so constantly, that at last Elsie grew desperate, got up, and went to the kitchen with a languid appeal, 'Please, Mrs Worrett, won't you let Johnnie stay by me, because my head aches so hard?' After that, Johnnie had rest; for Mrs Worrett was the kindest of women, and had no idea that she was not amusing her little guest in the most delightful manner.

A little before six, Elsie's head felt better; and she and Johnnie put on their hats, and went for a walk in the garden. There was not much to see: beds of vegetables, a few currant bushes, that was all. Elsie was leaning against a paling, and trying to make out why the Worrett house had that queer tiptoe expression, when a sudden loud grunt startled her, and something touched the top of her head. She turned, and there was an enormous pig standing on his hind legs on the other side of the paling. He was taller than Elsie as he stood thus, and it was his cold nose which had touched her head. Somehow, appearing in this unexpected way, he seemed to the children like some dreadful wild beast. They screamed with fright, and fled to the house, from which Elsie never ventured to stir again during their visit. John chased chickens at intervals, but it was a doubtful pleasure; and all the time she kept a wary eye on the distant pig.

That evening, while Mrs Worrett slept and Mr Worrett smoked outside the door, Elsie felt so very miserable that she broke down altogether. She put her head in Johnnie's lap, as they sat together in the darkest corner of the room, and sobbed and cried, making as little noise as she possibly could. Johnnie comforted her with soft pats and strokings; but did not dare to say a word, for fear Mrs Worrett should wake up and find them out.

When the morning came, Elsie's one thought was, would Alexander come for them in the afternoon? All day she watched the clock and the road with feverish anxiety. Oh, if papa had changed his mind, had decided to let them stay for a week at Conic Section, what should she do? It was just possible to worry through and keep alive till afternoon, she thought; but if they were forced to spend another night in that feather-bed, with those mosquitoes, hearing the blue shade rattle and quiver hour after hour, she should die, she was sure she should die!

But Elsie was not called upon to die, or even to discover how easy it is to survive a little discomfort. About five, her anxious watch was rewarded by the appearance of a cloud of dust, out of which presently emerged old Whitey's ears and the top of the well-known carriage. They stopped at the gate. There was Alexander, brisk and smiling, very glad to see his 'little misses again', and to find them so glad to go home. Mrs Worrett, however, did not discover that they were glad – no, indeed! Elsie and John were much too polite for that. They thanked the old lady, and said good-bye so prettily that, after they were gone, she told Mr Worrett that it hadn't been a bit of trouble having them there, and she hoped they would come again, they enjoyed everything so much; only it was a pity that Elsie looked so peaked. And at that very moment Elsie was sitting on the floor of the vehicle with her head in John's lap, crying and sobbing for joy that the visit was over, and that she was on the way home. 'If only I live to get there,' she said, 'I'll never, no, never, go into the country again!' which was silly enough; but we must forgive her.

Ah, how charming home did look, with the family grouped in the shady porch, Katy in her white wrapper, Clover with rose-buds in her belt, and everybody ready to welcome and pet the little absentees! There was much hugging and kissing, and much to tell of what had happened in the two days: how a letter had come from Cousin Helen; how Daisy White had four kittens as white as herself; how Dorry had finished his water-wheel – a wheel which turned in the bath-tub, and was 'really ingenious', papa said; and Phil had 'swapped' one of his bantam chicks for one of Eugene Slack's Brahmapootras. It was not till they were all seated round the tea-table that anybody demanded an account of the visit. Elsie felt this a relief, and was just thinking how delicious everything was, from the sliced peaches to the clinking ice in the milk-pitcher, when papa put the dreaded question –

'Well, Elsie, so you decided to come, after all. How was it? Why didn't you stay your week out? You look pale, it seems to me. Have you been enjoying yourself too much? Tell us all about it.'

Elsie looked at papa, and papa looked at Elsie. Dr Carr's eyes twinkled just a little, but otherwise he was perfectly grave. Elsie began to speak, then to laugh, then to cry, and the explanation, when it came, was given in a mingled burst of all three.

'O papa, it was horrid! That is, Mrs Worrett was just as kind as could be, but so fat; and oh, such a pig! I never imagined such a pig. And the calico on that horrid sofa was so slippery that I rolled off five times, and once

I hurt myself very badly. And we had a feather-bed; and I was so homesick that I cried all the evening.'

'That must have been gratifying to Mrs Worrett,' put in Dr Carr.

'Oh! she didn't know it, papa. She was asleep, and snoring so that nobody could hear. And the flies! – such flies, Katy! – and the mosquitoes, and our window wouldn't open till I put in a nail. I am so glad to get home! I never want to go into the country again, never, never! Oh, if Alexander hadn't come – why, Clover, what are you laughing for? And Dorry, I think it's very unkind,' and Elsie ran to Katy, hid her face, and began to cry.

'Never mind, darling, they didn't mean to be unkind. Papa, her hands are quite hot; you must give her something.' Katy's voice shook a little; but she would not hurt Elsie's feelings by showing that she was amused. Papa gave Elsie 'something' before she went to bed – a very mild dose, I fancy; for doctors' little girls, as a general rule, do take no medicine, and next day she was much better. As the adventures of the Conic Section visit leaked out bit by bit, the family laughed till it seemed as if they would never stop. Phil was for ever enacting the pig, standing on his triumphant hind legs, and patting Elsie's head with his nose; and many and many a time, 'It will end like your visit to Mrs Worrett' proved a useful check when Elsie was in self-willed mood and bent on some scheme which for the moment struck her as delightful. For one of the good things about our childish mistakes is, that each one teaches us something; and so, blundering on, we grow wiser, till, when the time comes, we are ready to take our places among the wonderful grown-up people who never make mistakes.

CHAPTER
2

A New Year
and a New Plan

When summer lingers on into October, it often seems as if winter, anxious to catch a glimpse of her, hurries a little; and so people are cheated out of their autumn. It was so that year. Almost as soon as it ceased to be hot, it began to be cold. The leaves, instead of drifting away in soft, dying colours, like sunset clouds, turned yellow all at once; and were whirled off the trees in a single gusty night, leaving everything bare and desolate. Thanksgiving came; and before the smell of the turkey was fairly out of the house, it was time to hang up stockings and dress the Christmas-tree. They had a tree that year in honour of Katy's being downstairs. Cecy, who had gone away to boarding-school, came home; and it was all delightful, except that the days flew too fast. Clover said it seemed to her very queer that there was so much less time than usual in the world. She couldn't imagine what had become of it; there used to be plenty. And she was certain that Dorry must have been tinkering with all the clocks – they struck so often.

It was just after New Year that Dr Carr walked in one

day with a letter in his hand, and remarked, 'Mr and Mrs Page are coming to stay with us.'

'Mr and Mrs Page,' repeated Katy: 'did I ever see them?'

'Once, when you were four years old, and Elsie a baby. Of course you don't remember it.'

'But who are they, papa?'

'Mrs Page was your dear mother's second cousin; and at one time she lived in your grandfather's family, and was like a sister to mamma and Uncle Charles. It is a good many years since I have seen her. Mr Page is a railroad engineer. He is coming this way on business, and they will stop for a few days with us. Your Cousin Olivia writes that she is anxious to see all you children. Have everything as nice as you can, Katy.'

'Of course, I will. What day are they coming?'

'Thursday – no, Friday,' replied Dr Carr, consulting the letter, 'Friday evening, at half-past six. Order something substantial for tea that night, Katy. They'll be hungry after travelling.'

Katy worked with a will for the next two days. Twenty times, at least, she went into the blue-room to make sure that nothing was forgotten; repeating, as if it had been a lesson in geography, 'Bath towels, face towels, matches, soap, candles, cologne, extra blanket, ink.' A nice little fire was lighted in the bedroom on Friday afternoon, and a big, beautiful one in the parlour, which looked very pleasant with the lamp lit and Clover's geraniums and china roses in the window. The tea-table was set with the best linen and the pink and white china. Debby's muffins were very light. The crab-apple jelly came out of its mould clear and whole, and the cold chicken looked appetizing, with its green wreath of parsley. There was stewed potato, too, and, of course, oysters. Everybody in Burnet had oysters for tea when company was expected. They were counted a special treat; because they were rather dear, and could not always be procured. Burnet was a thousand miles from the sea, so the oysters were of the tin-can variety. The cans gave the oysters a curious taste – tinny, or was it more like solder? At all events, Burnet people liked it, and always insisted that it was a striking improvement on the flavour which oysters have on their native shores. Everything was as nice as could be when Katy stood in the dining-room to take a last look at her arrangements; and she hoped papa would be pleased, and that mamma's cousin would think her a good housekeeper.

'I don't want to have on my other jacket,' observed Phil, putting his head in at the door. 'Need I? This is nice.'

'Let me see,' said Katy, gently turning him round. 'Well, it does pretty well; but I think I'd rather you should put on the other, if you don't mind much. We want everything as nice as possible, you know; because this is papa's company, and he hardly ever has any.'

'Just one little sticky place isn't much,' said Phil, rather gloomily, wetting his finger and rubbing at a shiny place on his sleeve. 'Do you really think I'd better? Well, then, I will.'

'That's a dear' – kissing him. 'Be quick, Philly, for it's almost time they were here. And please tell Dorry to make haste. It's ever so long since he went upstairs.'

'Dorry's an awful dandy,' remarked Phil, confidentially. 'He looks in the glass, and makes faces if he can't get his parting straight. I wouldn't care so much about my clothes for a good deal. It's like a girl. Jim Slack says a boy who shines his hair up like that never'll get to be President, not if he lives a thousand years.'

'Well,' said Katy, laughing; 'it's something to be clean, even if you cannot be President.'

She was not at all alarmed by Dorry's recent reaction in favour of personal adornment. He came down pretty soon, very spick and span in his best suit, and asked her to fasten the blue ribbon under his collar, which she did most obligingly; though he was very particular as to the size of the bows and length of the ends, and made her tie and re-tie more than once. She had just arranged it to suit him when a carriage stopped.

'There they are,' she cried. 'Run and open the door, Dorry.'

Dorry did so; and Katy, following, found papa ushering in a tall gentleman, and a lady who was not tall, but whose Roman nose and long neck, and general air of style and fashion, made her look so. Katy bent quite over to be kissed; but for all that she felt small, and young, and unformed, as the eyes of mamma's cousin looked her over and over, and through and through, and Mrs Page said –

'Why, Philip, is it possible that this tall girl is one of yours? Dear me! how the time flies! I was thinking of the little creatures I saw when I was here last. And this other great creature can't be Elsie? That mite of a baby! Impossible! I cannot realize it. I really cannot realize it in the least.'

'Won't you come to the fire, Mrs Page?' said Katy, rather timidly.

'Don't call me Mrs Page, my dear. Call me Cousin Olivia.'

Then the newcomer rustled into the parlour, where Johnnie and Phil were waiting to be introduced; and again she remarked that she 'couldn't realize it.' I don't know why Mrs Page's not realizing it should have made Katy uncomfortable, but it did.

Supper went off well. The guests ate and praised; and Dr Carr looked pleased, and said: 'We think Katy an excellent housekeeper for her age.' At which Katy blushed and was delighted, till she caught Mrs Page's eyes fixed upon her with a look of scrutiny and amusement, whereupon she felt awkward and ill at ease.

It was so all the evening. Mamma's cousin was entertaining and bright, and told lively stories; but the children felt that she was watching them, and passing judgment on their ways. Children are very quick to suspect when older people hold within themselves these little private courts of inquiry, and they always resent it.

Next morning Mrs Page sat by while Katy washed the breakfast things, fed the birds, and did various odd jobs about the room and house.

'My dear,' she said at last, 'what a solemn girl you are! I should think from your face that you were at least five-and-thirty. Don't you ever laugh or frolic, like other girls of your age? Why, my Lilly, who is four months older than you, is a perfect child still; impulsive as a baby, bubbling over with fun from morning till night.'

'I've been shut up a good deal,' said Katy, trying to defend herself; 'but I didn't know I was solemn.'

'My dear, that's the very thing I complain of; you don't know it! You are altogether ahead of your age. It's very bad for you, in my opinion. All this housekeeping and care, for young girls like you and Clover, is wrong and unnatural. I don't like it; indeed I don't.'

'Oh! housekeeping doesn't hurt me a bit,' protested Katy, trying to smile. 'We have lovely times; indeed we do, Cousin Olivia.'

Cousin Olivia only pursed up her mouth, and repeated, 'It's wrong, my dear. It's unnatural. It's not the thing for you. Depend upon it, it's not the thing.'

This was unpleasant; but what was worse, had Katy known it, Mrs Page attacked Dr Carr upon the subject. He was quite troubled to learn that she considered Katy grave and careworn, and unlike what girls of her age should be. Katy caught him looking at her with a puzzled expression.

'What is it, dear papa? Do you want anything?'

'No, child, nothing. What are you doing there? Mending the parlour curtain, eh? Can't old Mary attend to that, and give you a chance to frisk about with the other girls?'

'Papa! As if I wanted to frisk! I declare you're as bad as Cousin Olivia. She's always telling me that I ought to bubble over with mirth. I don't wish to bubble. I don't know how.'

'I'm afraid you don't,' said Dr Carr, with an odd sigh, which set Katy to wondering. What should papa sigh for? Had she done anything wrong? She began to rack her brains and memory as to whether it could be this or that; or, if not, what could it be? Such needless self-examination does no good. Katy looked 'more solemn' than ever after it.

Altogether, Mrs Page was not a favourite in the family.

She had every intention of being kind to her cousin's children, 'so dreadfully in want of a mother, poor things!' but she could not hide the fact that their ways puzzled and did not please her, and the children detected this, as children always will. She and Mr Page were very polite. They praised the housekeeping, and the excellent order of everything, and said that there never were better children in the world than John, and Dorry, and Phil. But, through all, Katy perceived the hidden disapproval; and she couldn't help feeling glad when the visit ended, and they went away.

With their departure, matters went back to their old train, and Katy forgot her disagreeable feelings. Papa seemed a little grave and preoccupied; but doctors often are when they have bad cases to think of, and nobody noticed it particularly, or remarked that several letters came from Mrs Page, and nothing was heard of their contents, except that 'Cousin Olivia sent her love'. So it was a shock, when one day papa called Katy into the study to tell her of a new plan. She knew at once that it was something important when she heard his voice; it sounded so grave. Besides, he said, 'My daughter' – a phrase he never used except upon the most impressive occasions.

'My daughter,' he began, 'I want to talk to you about something which I have been thinking of. How would you and Clover like going away to school together?'

'To school? To Mrs Knight's?'

'No, not to Mrs Knight's. To a boarding-school at the East, where Lilly Page has been for two years. Didn't you hear Cousin Olivia speak of it when she was here?'

'I believe I did. But, papa, you won't really?'

'Yes, I think so,' said Dr Carr, gently. 'Listen, Katy,

and don't feel so badly, my dear child. I've thought the plan over carefully; and it seems to me a good one, though I hate to part from you. It is pretty much as your cousin says; these home cares, which I can't take from you while you are at home, are making you old before your time. Heaven knows, I don't want to turn you into a silly, giggling miss; but I should like you to enjoy your youth while you have it, and not grow middle-aged before you are twenty.'

'What is the name of the school?' asked Katy. Her voice sounded a good deal like a sob.

'The girls call it "The Nunnery". It is at Hillsover, on the Connecticut River, pretty far north. And the winters are pretty cold, I fancy; but the air is sure to be good and bracing. That is one thing which has inclined me to the plan. The climate is just what you need.'

'Hillsover? Isn't there a college there, too?'

'Yes; Arrowmouth College. I believe there is always a college where there is a boarding-school; though why, I can't for the life of me imagine. That's neither here nor there, however, I'm not afraid of your getting into silly scrapes, as girls sometimes do.'

'College scrapes? Why, how could I? We don't have anything to do with the college, do we?' said Katy, opening her candid eyes with such a wondering stare, that Dr Carr laughed, as he patted her cheek, and replied, 'No, my dear, not a thing.'

'The term opens the third week in April,' he went on. 'You must begin to get ready at once. Mrs Hall has just fitted out Cecy; so she can tell you what you will need. You'd better consult her tomorrow.'

'But, papa,' cried Katy, beginning to realize it, 'what

are you going to do? Elsie's a darling, but she's so very little. I don't see how you can possibly manage. I'm sure you'll miss us, and so will the children.'

'I rather think we shall,' said Dr Carr, with a smile, which ended with a sigh; 'but we shall do very well, Katy; never fear. Miss Finch will see to us.'

'Miss Finch? Do you mean Mrs Knight's sister-in-law?'

'Yes. Her mother died in the summer; so she has no particular home now, and is glad to come for a year and keep house for us. Mrs Knight says she is a good manager; and I dare say she'll fill your place sufficiently well, as far as that goes. We can't expect her to be *you*, you know: that would be unreasonable.' And Dr Carr put his arm round Katy, and kissed her so fondly that she was quite overcome, and clung to him, crying –

'O papa! don't make us go. I'll frisk, and be as young as I can, and not grow middle-aged or anything disagreeable, if only you'll let us stay. Never mind what Cousin Olivia says; she doesn't know. Cousin Helen wouldn't say so, I'm sure.'

'On the contrary, Helen thinks well of the plan; only she wishes the school were nearer,' said Dr Carr. 'No, Katy, don't coax. My mind is made up. It will do you and Clover both good; and once you are settled at Hillsover, you'll be very happy, I hope.'

When papa spoke in this decided tone, it was never any use to urge him. Katy knew this, and ceased her pleadings. She went to find Clover and tell her the news, and the two girls had a hearty cry together. A sort of 'clearing-up shower' it turned out to be; for when once they had wiped their eyes, everything looked brighter, and they began to see a pleasant side to the plan.

'The travelling part of it will be very nice,' pronounced Clover. 'We never went so far away from home before.'

Elsie, who was still looking very woeful, burst into tears afresh at this remark.

'Oh, don't darling!' said Katy. 'Think how pleasant it will be to send letters, and to get them from us. I shall write to you every Saturday. Run for the big atlas – there's a dear, and let us see where we are going.'

Elsie brought the atlas; and the three heads bent eagerly over it, as Clover traced the route of the journey with her forefinger. How exciting it looked! There was the railroad, twisting and curving over half-a-dozen States. The black dots which followed it were towns and villages, all of which they should see. By and by the road made a bend, and swept northward by the side of the Connecticut River and toward the hills. They had heard how beautiful the Connecticut valley is.

'Only think! we shall be close to it,' remarked Clover; 'and we shall see the hills. I suppose they are very high, a great deal higher than the hill at Bolton.'

'I hope so,' laughed Dr Carr, who came into the room just then. The hill at Bolton was one of his favourite jokes. When mamma first came to Burnet, she had paid a visit to some friends at Bolton; and one day, when they were all out walking, they asked her if she felt strong enough to go to the top of the hill. Mamma was used to hills, so she said yes, and walked on, very glad to find that there was a hill in that flat country, but wondering a little why they did not see it. At last she asked where it was, and, behold, they had just reached the top! The slope had been so gradual that she had never found out that they were going uphill at all. Dr Carr had told this story to the children, but had never been able to make them see the joke very clearly. In fact, when Clover went to Bolton, she was quite struck with the hill: it was so much higher than the sandbank which bordered the lake at Burnet.

There was a great deal to do to make the girls ready for school by the third week in April. Mrs Hall was very kind, and her advice was sensible; though, except for Dr Carr, the girls would hardly have had furs and flannels enough for so cold a place as Hillsover. Everything for winter, as well as for summer, had to be thought of; for it had been arranged that the girls should not come home for the autumn vacation, but should spend it with Mrs Page. This was the hardest thing about the plan. Katy begged very hard for Christmas; but when she learned that it would take three days to come and three to go, and that the holidays lasted less than a week, she saw it was of no use, and gave up the idea, while Elsie tried to comfort herself by planning a Christmas box. The preparations kept them so busy that there was no time for anything else. Mrs Hall was always wanting them to go with her to shops, or Miss Petingill demanding that they should try on linings; and so the days flew by. At last all was ready. The nice halfdozens of pretty underclothes came home from the sewing-machine woman's, and were done up by Bridget, who dropped many a tear into the starch at the thought of the young ladies going away. Mrs Hall, who was a good packer, put the things into the new trunks. Everybody gave the girls presents, as if they had been brides starting on a wedding journey.

Papa's was a watch for each. They were not new, but the girls thought them beautiful. Katy's had belonged to her mother. It was large and old-fashioned, with a finely-wrought case. Clover's, which had been her grandmother's, was larger still. It had a quaint ornament on the back – a sort of true-love knot, done in gold of different tints. The girls were excessively pleased with these watches. They wore them with guard-chains of black watered ribbon, and every other minute they looked to see what the time was.

Elsie had been in papa's confidence, so her presents were watchcases, embroidered on perforated paper. Johnnie gave Katy a box of pencils, and Clover a pen-knife with a pearl handle. Dorry and Phil clubbed to buy a box of notepaper and envelopes, which the girls were requested to divide between them. Miss Petingill contributed a bottle of ginger balsam, and a box of opodeldoc salve, to be used in case of possible chilblains. Old Mary's offering was a couple of needle-books, full of bright, sharp needles.

'I wouldn't give you scissors,' she said; 'but you can't cut love – or, for the matter of that, anything else – with a needle.'

Miss Finch, the new housekeeper, arrived a few days before they started: so Katy had time to take her over the house and explain all the different things she wanted done and not done to secure papa's comfort and the children's. Miss Finch was meek and gentle. She seemed glad of a comfortable home. And Katy felt that she would be kind to the boys, and not fret Debby, and drive her into marrying Alexander and going away – an event which Aunt Izzie had been used to predict. Now that all was settled, she and Clover found themselves looking forward to the change with pleasure. There was something new and interesting about it which excited their imaginations.

The last evening was a melancholy one. Elsie had been too much absorbed in the preparations to realize her loss;

but when it came to locking the trunks, her courage gave way altogether. She was in such a state of affliction that everybody else became afflicted too; and there is no knowing what would have happened, had not a parcel arrived by express and distracted their attention. The parcel was from Cousin Helen, whose things, like herself, had a knack of coming at the moment when most wanted. It contained two pretty silk umbrellas – one brown, and one dark green, with Katy's initials on one handle, and Clover's on the other. Opening these treasures, and exclaiming over them, helped the family through the evening wonderfully; the next morning there was such a bustle of getting off that nobody had time to cry.

After the last kisses had been given, and Philly, who had climbed on the horse-block, was clamouring for 'one more – just one more', Dr Carr, looking at the sober faces, was struck by a bright idea; and calling Alexander, told him to hurry old Whitey into the carriage, and drive the children down to Willett's Point, that they might wave their handkerchiefs to the boat as she went by. This suggestion worked like a charm on the spirits of the party. Phil began to caper, and Elsie and John ran in to get their hats. Half an hour later, when the boat rounded the point, there stood the little crew, radiant with smiles, fluttering their handkerchiefs and kissing their hands as cheerfully as possible. It was a pleasant last look to the two who stood beside papa on the deck; and, as they waved back their greetings to the little ones, and then looked forward across the blue water tò ìhe unknown places they were going to see, Katy and Clover felt that the new life opened well, and promised to be very interesting indeed.

CHAPTER
3

ON THE WAY

The journey from Burnet to Hillsover was a very long one. It took the greater part of three days, and as Dr Carr was in a hurry to get back to his patients, they travelled without stopping; spending the first night on the boat, and the second on a railroad train. Papa found this tiresome; but the girls, to whom everything was new, thought it delightful. They enjoyed their stateroom, with its narrow shelves of beds, as much as if it had been a baby-house, and they two children playing in it. To tuck themselves away for the night in a car-section seemed the greatest fun in the world. When older people fretted, they laughed. Everything was interesting, from the telegraph-poles by the wayside, to the faces of their fellow-passengers. It amused them to watch strange people, and make up stories about them – where they were going, and what relation they could be to each other. The strange people, in their turn, cast curious glances toward the bright, happy-faced sisters; but Katy and Clover did not mind that, or, in fact, notice it. They were too much absorbed to think of themselves, or the impression they were making on others.

It was early on the third morning that the train, puffing and shrieking, ran into the Springfield depot. Other trains stood waiting; and there was such a chorus of snorts and whistles, and such clouds of smoke, that Katy was half frightened. Papa, who was half asleep, jumped up, and told the girls to collect their bags and books; for they were to breakfast here, and to meet Lilly Page, who was going on to Hillsover with them.

'Do you suppose she is here already?' asked Katy, tucking the railway-guide into the shawl-strap, and closing her bag with a snap.

'Yes; we shall meet her at the Massasoit. She and her father were to pass the night there.'

The Massasoit was close at hand, and in less than five minutes the girls and papa were seated at a table in its pleasant dining-room. They were ordering their breakfast, when Mr Page came in, accompanied by his daughter – a pretty girl, with light hair, delicate, rather sharp features, and her mother's stylish ease of manner. Her travelling-dress was simple, but had the finish which a French dressmaker knows how to give a simple thing; and all its appointments – boots, hat, gloves, collar, neck ribbon – were so perfect, each in its way, that Clover, glancing down at her own grey alpaca, and then at Katy's, felt suddenly countrified and shabby.

'Well, Lilly, here they are; here are your cousins,' said Mr Page, giving the girls a cordial greeting. Lilly only said, 'How do you do?' Clover saw her glancing at the grey alpacas, and was conscious of a sudden flush. But perhaps Lilly looked at something beside the alpaca; for after a minute her manner changed, and became more friendly.

'Did you order waffles?' she asked.

'Waffles? no, I think not,' replied Katy.

'Oh! why not? Don't you know how celebrated they are for waffles at this hotel? I thought everybody knew *that*.' Then she tinkled her fork against her glass, and when the waiter came, said, 'Waffles, please,' with an air which impressed Clover extremely. Lilly seemed to her like a young lady in a story, so elegant and self-possessed. She wondered if all the girls at Hillsover were going to be like her.

The waffles came, crisp and hot, with delicious maple syrup to eat on them; and the party made a satisfactory breakfast. Lilly, in spite of all her elegance, displayed a wonderful appetite. 'You see,' she explained to Clover, 'I don't expect to have another decent thing to eat till next September – not a thing, so I'm making the most of this.' Accordingly she disposed of nine waffles in quick succession, before she found time to utter anything further, except, 'Butter, please,' or, 'May I trouble you for the molasses?' As she swallowed the last morsel, Dr Carr, looking at his watch, said that it was time to start for the train; and they set off. Mr Page went with them. As they crossed the street, Katy was surprised to see that Lilly, who had seemed quite happy only a minute before, had begun to cry. After they reached the car, her tears increased to sobs; she grew almost hysterical.

'Oh! don't make me go, papa,' she implored, clinging to her father's arm. 'I shall be so homesick! It will kill me, I know it will. Please let me stay. Please let me go home with you.'

'Now, my darling,' protested Mr Page, 'this is foolish: you know it is.'

'I can't help it,' blubbered Lilly. 'I ca – n't help it. Oh! don't, don't make me go. Don't, papa, dear. I ca – n't bear it.'

Katy and Clover felt embarrassed during this scene. They had always been used to considering tears as things to be rather ashamed of – to be kept back, if possible; or, if not, shed in private corners, in dark closets, or behind the bed in the nursery. To see the stylish Lilly crying like a baby, in the midst of the railway carriage, with strangers looking on, quite shocked them. It did not last long however. The whistle sounded, the conductor shouted, 'All right!' and Mr Page, giving Lilly a last kiss, disengaged her clinging arms, put her into the seat beside Clover, and hurried out of the car. Lilly sobbed loudly for a few seconds; then she dried her eyes, lifted her head, adjusted her veil and the wrists of her three-buttoned gloves, and remarked –

'I always go on in this way. Ma says I am a real cry-baby; and I suppose I am. I don't see how people can be calm and composed when they're leaving home, do you? You'll be just as bad tomorrow, when you come to say good-bye to your papa.'

'Oh! I hope not,' said Katy. 'Because papa would feel so badly.'

Lilly stared. 'I shall think you real cold-hearted if you don't,' she said, in an offended tone.

Katy took no notice of the tone; and before long Lilly recovered from her pettishness, and began to talk about the school. Katy and Clover asked eager questions. They were eager to hear all that Lilly could tell.

'You'll adore Mrs Florence,' she said, 'All the girls do. She's the most fascinating woman! She does just what she likes with everybody. Why, even the students think her perfectly splendid; and yet she's just as strict as she can be.'

'Strict with students?' asked Clover, looking puzzled.

'No; strict with us girls. She never lets any one call, unless it's a brother or a first cousin; and then you must have a letter from your parents, asking permission. I wanted ma to write and say that George Hickman might call on me. He isn't a first cousin exactly, but his father married pa's sister-in-law's sister. So it's just as good. But ma was real mean about it. She says I'm too young to have gentlemen coming to see me! I can't think why. Ever so many girls who are younger than I have 'em. Which row are you going to sleep in?' she went on.

'I don't know. Nobody told us that there were any rows.'

'Oh, yes! Shaker Row, and Quaker Row, and Attic Row. Attic Row is the nicest, because it's highest up, and furthest away from Mrs Florence. My room is in Attic Row. Annie Silsbie and I engaged it last term. You'll be in Quaker Row, I guess. Most of the new girls are.'

'Is that a nice row?' asked Clover, greatly interested.

'Pretty nice. It isn't so good as Attic, but it's very much better than Shaker; because there you're close to Mrs Florence, and can't have a bit of fun without her hearing you. I'd try to get the end room, if I were you. Mary Andrews and I had it once. There is a splendid view of Berry Searles's windows.'

'Berry Searles?'

'Yes; President Searles, you know; his youngest son. He's an elegant fellow. All the girls are cracked about him – perfectly cracked! The President's house is next door to the Nunnery, you know; and Berry rooms at the very end of the back building, just opposite Quaker Row. It used to be such fun! He'd sit at his window, and we'd sit at ours, in silent study hour, you know; and he'd pretend to read, and all the time keep looking over the top of his book at us, and trying to make us laugh. Once Mary did laugh right out; and Miss Jane heard her, and came in. But Berry is just as quick as a flash, and he ducked down under the window-sill; so she didn't see him. It was such fun!'

'Who's Miss Jane?' asked Katy.

'The horridest old thing. She's Mrs Florence's niece, and engaged to a missionary. Mrs Florence keeps her on purpose to spy on us girls, and report when we break the rules. Oh, those rules! Just wait till you come to read 'em over. They're nailed up on all the doors – thirty-two of them – and you can't help breaking 'em if you try ever so much.'

'What are they? what sort of rules?' cried Katy and Clover in a breath.

'Oh! about being punctual to prayers, and turning your mattress, and smoothing over the under-sheet before you leave your room, and never speaking a word in the hall, or in private-study hour, and hanging your towel on your own nail in the wash-room, and all that.'

'Wash-room? what do you mean?' said Katy, aghast.

'At the head of Quaker Row, you know. All the girls wash there, except on Saturdays, when they go to the bath-house. You have your own bowl and soap-dish, and a hook for your towel. Why, what's the matter? How big your eyes are!'

'I never heard anything so horrid!' cried Katy, when she had recovered her breath. 'Do you really mean that the girls don't have wash-stands in their own rooms?'

'You'll get used to it. All the girls do,' responded Lilly.

'I don't want to get used to it,' said Katy, resolving to appeal to papa; but papa had gone into the smoking-car, and she had to wait. Meantime Lilly went on talking.

'If you have that end room in Quaker Row, you'll see all the fun that goes on at commencement time. Mrs Searles always has a big party, and you can look right in, and watch the people and the supper-table, just as if you were there. Last summer Berry and Alpheus Seccomb got a lot of cakes and mottoes from the table and came out into the yard, and threw them up one by one to Rose Red and her room-mate. They didn't have the end room, though; but the one next to it.'

'What a funny name! – Rose Red,' said Clover.

'Oh! her real name is Rosamund Redding; but the girls call her Rose Red. She's the greatest witch in the school; not exactly pretty, you know, but sort of killing and fascinating. She's always getting into the most awful scrapes. Mrs Florence would have expelled her long ago if she hadn't been such a favourite; and Mr Redding's daughter, beside. He's a member of Congress, you know, and all that; and Mrs Florence is quite proud of having Rose in her school.

'Berry Searles is so funny!' she continued. 'His mother is a horrid old thing, and always interfering with him. Sometimes when he has a party of fellows in his room, and they're playing cards, we can see her coming with her candle through the house; and when she gets to his door, she tries it, and then she knocks, and calls out, "Abernethy, my son!" And the fellows whip the cards into their pockets, and stick the bottles under the table and get out their books and dictionaries in a minute; and when Berry unlocks the door, there they sit, studying away; and Mrs Searles looks so disappointed! I thought I should die one night, me and Mary Andrews laughed so.'

I verily believe that if Dr Carr had been present at this conversation, he would have stopped at the next station, and taken the girls back to Burnet. But he did not return from the smoking-car till the anecdotes about Berry were finished, and Lilly had begun again on Mrs Florence.

'She's a sort of queen, you know. Everybody minds her. She's tall, and always dresses beautifully. Her eyes are lovely; but, when she gets angry, they're perfectly awful. Rose Red says she'd rather face a mad bull any day than Mrs Florence in a fury; and Rose ought to know, for she's had more reprimands than any girl in the school.'

'How many girls are there?' inquired Dr Carr.

'There were forty-eight last term. I don't know how many there'll be this, for they say Mrs Florence is going to give up. It's she who makes the school so popular.'

All this time the train was moving northward. With every mile the country grew prettier. Spring had not fairly opened; but the grass was green, and the buds on the trees gave a tender mist-like colour to the woods. The road followed the river, which here and there turned upon itself in long links and windings. Ranges of blue hills closed the distance. Now and then a nearer mountain rose, single and alone, from the plain. The air was cool, and full of a brilliant zest, which the Western girls had never before tasted. Katy felt as if she were drinking champagne. She and Clover flew from window to window, exclaiming with such delight that Lilly was surprised.

'I can't see what there is to make such a fuss about,' she remarked. 'That's only Deerfield. It's quite a small place.'

'But how pretty it looks, nestled in among the hills! Hills are lovely, Clover, aren't they?'

'These hills are nothing. You should see the White Mountains,' said the experienced Lilly. 'Ma and me spent three weeks at the Profile House last vacation. It was perfectly elegant.'

In the course of the afternoon Katy drew papa away to a distant seat, and confided her distress about the wash-stands.

'Don't you think it is horrid, pa? Aunt Izzie always said it isn't lady-like not to take a sponge-bath every morning; but how can we, with forty-eight girls in the room? I don't see what we are going to do.'

'I fancy we can arrange it; don't be distressed, my dear,' replied Dr Carr. And Katy was satisfied; for when papa undertook to arrange things, they were very apt to be done.

It was almost evening when they reached their final stopping-place.

'Now, two miles in the stage, and then we're at the horrid old Nunnery,' said Lilly. 'Ugh! look at that snow. It never melts here till long after it's all gone at home.

How I do hate this station! I'm going to be frightfully homesick: I know I am.'

But just then she caught sight of the stagecoach, which stood waiting, and her mood changed: for the stage was full of girls who had come by the other train.

'Hurrah! there's Mary Edwards and Mary Silver,' she exclaimed; 'and, I declare, Rose Red! Oh, you precious darling! how do you do?' Scrambling up the steps, she plunged at a girl with waving hair, and a rosy, mischievous face; and began kissing her with effusion.

Rose Red did not seem equally enchanted. 'Well, Lilly, how are you?' she said, and then went on talking to a girl who sat by her side, and whose hand she held; while Lilly rushed up and down the line, embracing and being embraced. She did not introduce Katy and Clover; and, as papa was outside, on the driver's box, they felt a little lonely and strange. All the rest were chattering merrily, and were evidently well acquainted: they were the only ones left out.

Clover watched Rose Red, to whose face she had taken a fancy. It made her think of a pink carnation, or of a twinkling wild rose, with saucy whiskers of brown calyx. Whatever she said or did seemed full of a flavour especially her own. Her eyes, which were blue and not very large, sparkled with fun and mischief. Her cheeks were round and soft, like a baby's: when she laughed, two dimples broke their pink, and made you want to laugh too. A cunning white throat supported this pretty head, as a stem supports a flower; and, altogether, she was like a flower, except that flowers don't talk, and she talked all the time. What she said seemed very droll, for the girls about her were in fits of laughter; but Clover only caught a word now and then, the stage made such a noise.

Suddenly Rose Red leaned forward, and touched Clover's hand.

'What's your name?' she said. 'You've got eyes like my sister's. Are you coming to the Nunnery?'

'Yes,' replied Clover, smiling back. 'My name is Clover – Clover Carr.'

'What a dear little name! It sounds just as you look!'

'So does your name – Rose Red,' said Clover shyly.

'It's a ridiculous name,' protested Rose Red, trying to pout.

Just then the stage stopped.

'Why? Who's going to the hotel?' cried the school-girls in a chorus.

'I am,' said Dr Carr, putting his head in at the door, with a smile which captivated every girl there. 'Come, Katy; come, Clover. I've decided that you shan't begin school till tomorrow.'

'Oh, my! Don't I wish he was my pa!' cried Rose Red. Then the stage moved on.

'Who are they? What's their name?' asked the girls. 'They look nice.'

'They're sort of cousins of mine, and they come from the West,' replied Lilly, not unwilling to own the relationship, now that she perceived that Dr Carr had made a favourable impression.

'Why on earth didn't you introduce them, then? I declare that was just like you, Lilly Page,' put in Rose Red, indignantly. ''They looked so lonesome that I wanted to pat and stroke both of 'em. That little one has the sweetest eyes!'

Meantime Katy and Clover entered the hotel, very glad of the reprieve, and of one more quiet evening alone with papa. They needed to get their ideas straightened out and put to rights after the confusions of the day and Lilly's extraordinary talk. It was very evident that the Nunnery was to be quite different from their expectations; but another thing was equally evident – it would not be dull! Rose Red by herself, and without any one to help her, would be enough to prevent that!

CHAPTER
4

THE NUNNERY

The night seemed short; for the girls, tired by their journey, slept like dormice. About seven o'clock Katy was roused by the click of a blind; and, opening her eyes, saw Clover standing in the window, and peeping out through the half-opened shutters. When she heard Katy move, she cried out –

'Oh, do come! It's so interesting! I can see the colleges and the church, and, I guess, the Nunnery; only I am not quite sure, because the houses are all so much alike.'

Katy jumped up and hurried to the window. The hotel stood on one side of a green common, planted with trees. The common had a lead-coloured fence, and gravel paths, which ran across it from corner to corner. Opposite the hotel was a long row of red buildings, broken by one or two brown ones, with cupolas. These were evidently the colleges, and a large grey building with a spire was as evidently the church; but which one of the many white, green-blinded houses which filled the other sides of the common, was the Nunnery, the girls could not tell. Clover thought it was one with a garden at the side; but Katy thought not, because Lilly had said nothing of a garden. They discussed the point so long, that the breakfast-bell took them by surprise; and they were forced to rush through their dressing as fast as possible, so as not to keep papa waiting.

When breakfast was over, Dr Carr told them to put on their hats, and get ready to walk with him to the school. Clover took one arm, and Katy the other; and the three passed between some lead-coloured posts, and took one of the diagonal paths which led across the common.

'That's the house,' said Dr Carr, pointing.

'It isn't the one you picked out, Clover,' said Katy.

'No,' replied Clover, a little disappointed. The house papa indicated was by no means so pleasant as the one she had chosen.

It was a tall, narrow building, with dormer windows in the roof, and a square porch supported by whitewashed pillars. A pile of trunks stood in the porch. From above came sounds of voices. Girls' heads were popped out of upper windows at the swinging of the gate; and, as the door opened, more heads appeared looking over the balusters from the hall above.

The parlour into which they were taken was full of heavy, old-fashioned furniture, stiffly arranged. The sofa and chairs were covered with black haircloth, and stood closely against the wall. Some books lay upon the table, arranged two by two; each upper book being exactly at a right angle with each lower book. A bunch of dried grasses stood in the fire-place. There were no pictures, except one portrait in oils, of a forbidding old gentleman in a wig and glasses, sitting with his middle finger majestically inserted in a half-open Bible. Altogether, it was not a cheerful room, nor one calculated to raise the spirits of new-comers; and Katy, whose long seclusion had made her sensitive on the subject of rooms, shrank instinctively nearer papa as they went in.

Two ladies rose to receive them. One, a tall, dignified person, was Mrs Florence. The other she introduced as, 'My assistant principal, Mrs Nipson.' Mrs Nipson was not tall. She had a round face, pinched lips, and half-shut grey eyes.

'This lady is fully associated with me in the management of the school,' explained Mrs Florence. 'When I go, she will assume the entire control.'

'Is that likely to be soon?' inquired Dr Carr, surprised, and not well pleased that the teacher of whom he had heard, and with whom he had proposed to leave his children, was planning to yield her place to a stranger.

'The time is not yet determined,' replied Mrs Florence. Then she changed the subject – gracefully, but so decidedly, that Dr Carr had no chance for further question. She spoke of classes, and discussed what Katy and Clover were to study. Finally, she proposed to take them upstairs to see their room. Papa might come too, she said.

'I dare say that Lilly Page, who tells me that she is a cousin of yours, has described the arrangements of the house,' she remarked to Katy. 'The room I have assigned to you is in the back building. "Quaker Row", the girls call it.'

She smiled as she spoke; and Katy, meeting her eyes for the first time, felt that there was something in what Lilly had said, Mrs Florence *was* a sort of queen.

They went upstairs. Some girls, who were peeping over the baluster, hurried away at their approach. Mrs Florence shook her head at them.

'The first day is always one of licence,' she said, leading the way along an uncarpeted entry to a door at the end, from which, by a couple of steps, they went down into a square room – round three sides of which ran a shelf, on which stood rows of wash-bowls and pitchers. Above were hooks for towels. Katy perceived that this was the much-dreaded wash-room.

'Our lavatory,' remarked Mrs Florence, blandly. Opening from the wash-room was a very long hall, lighted at each end by a window. The doors on either side were numbered 'one, two, three,' and so on. Some of them were half open; as they went by, Katy and Clover caught glimpses of girls and trunks, and beds strewed with things. At No. 6 Mrs Florence paused.

'Here is the room which I propose to give you,' she said.

Katy and Clover looked eagerly about. It was a small room, but the sun shone in cheerfully at the window. There was a maple bedstead and table, a couple of chairs, and a row of hooks; that was all, except that in the wall was set a case of black-handled drawers, with cupboard-doors above them.

'These take the place of a bureau, and hold your clothes,' explained Mrs Florence, pulling out one of the drawers. 'I hope, when once you are settled, you will find yourselves comfortable. The rooms are small; but young people do not require so much space as older ones. Though, indeed, your elder daughter, Dr Carr, looks more advanced and grown up than I was prepared to find her. What did you say was her age?'

'She is past sixteen; but she has been so long confined to her room by the illness of which I wrote, that you may probably find her behindhand in some respects, which reminds me' (this was very adroit of papa!) 'I am anxious that she should keep up the system to which she has been accustomed at home – among other things, sponge-baths of cold water every morning; and, as I see that the bedrooms are not furnished with wash-stands, I will ask your permission to provide one for the use of my little girls. Perhaps you will kindly tell me where I had better look for it?'

Mrs Florence was not pleased, but she could not object, so she mentioned a shop. Katy's heart gave a bound of relief. She thought No. 6 with a wash-stand might be very comfortable. Its bareness and simplicity had the charm of novelty. Then there was something very interesting to her in the idea of a whole house full of girls.

They did not stay long after seeing the room, but went off on a shopping excursion. Shops were few and far between at Hillsover, but they found a neat little maple wash-stand and rocking-chair, and papa also bought a comfortable low chair, with a slatted back and a cushion. This was for Katy.

'Never study till your back aches,' he told her; 'when you are tired, lie flat on the bed for half an hour, and tell Mrs Florence that it was by my direction.'

'Or Mrs Nipson,' said Katy, laughing rather ruefully. She had taken no fancy to Mrs Nipson, and did not enjoy the idea of a divided authority.

A hurried lunch at the hotel followed, and then it was time for Dr Carr to go away. They all walked to the school together, and said good-bye on the steps. The girls would not cry, but they clung very tightly to papa, and put as much feeling into their last kisses as would have furnished forth half-a-dozen fits of tears. Lilly might have thought them cold-hearted, but papa did not; he knew better.

'That's my brave girls!' he said. Then he kissed them once more and hurried away. Perhaps he did not wish them to see that his eyes too were a little misty.

As the door closed behind them, Katy and Clover realized that they were alone among strangers. The sensation was not pleasant, and they felt forlorn as they went upstairs, and down Quaker Row, towards No. 6.

'Aha! so you're going to be next door,' said a gay voice, as they passed No. 5, and Rose Red popped her head into the hall. 'Well, I'm glad,' she went on, shaking hands cordially. 'I was in hopes you would, and yet I didn't know; and there are some awful stiffies among the new girls. How do you both do?'

'Oh, are we next door to you?' cried Clover, brightening.

'Yes. It's rather good of me not to hate you, for I wanted the end room myself, and Mrs Florence wouldn't give it to me. Come in, and let me introduce you to my room-mate. It's against the rules, but that's no matter; nobody pretends to keep rules the first day.'

They went in. No. 5 was precisely like No. 6 in shape, size, and furniture; but Rose had unpacked her trunk, and decorated her room with odds and ends of all sorts. The table was covered with books and boxes; coloured lithographs were pinned on the walls; a huge blue rosette ornamented the head-board of the bed; the blinds were tied together with pink ribbon; over the top of the window was a festoon of hemlock boughs, fresh and spicy. The effect was fantastic, but cheery, and Katy and Clover exclaimed with one voice, 'How pretty!'

The room-mate was a pale, shy girl, with a half-scared look in her eyes, and small hands which twisted uneasily together when she moved and spoke. Her name was Mary Silver. She and Rose were so utterly unlike, that Katy thought it odd that they should have chosen to be together. Afterwards she understood it better. Rose liked to protect, and Mary to be protected; Rose to talk, and Mary to listen. Mary evidently considered Rose the most entertaining creature in the world; she giggled violently at all her jokes, and then stopped short and covered her mouth with her fingers, in a frightened way, as if giggling were wrong.

'Only think, Mary,' began Rose, after introducing Katy and Clover, 'these young ladies have got the end room. What do you suppose was the reason that Mrs Florence did not give it to us? It's very peculiar.'

Mary laughed her uneasy laugh. She looked as if she could tell the reason, but did not dare.

'Never mind,' continued Rose. 'Trials are good for one, they say. It's something to have nice people in that room, if we can't be there ourselves. You are nice, aren't you?' turning to Clover.

'Very,' replied Clover, laughing.

'I thought so. I can almost always tell without asking; still, it is something to have it on the best authority. We'll be good neighbours, won't we? Look here,' and she pulled one of the black-handled drawers completely out and laid it on the bed. 'Do you see? your drawers are exactly behind ours. Any time in silent study hour, if I have something I want to say, I'll just rap and pop a note into your drawer, and you can do the same to me. Isn't it fun?'

Clover said, 'Yes'; but Katy, though she laughed, shook her head.

'Don't entice us into mischief,' she said.

'Oh, gracious!' exclaimed Rose. 'Now, are you going to be good, – you two? If you are, just break the news at once, and have it over. I can bear it.' She fanned herself in such a comical way that no one could help laughing. Mary Silver joined, but stopped pretty soon in her sudden manner.

'There's Mary, now,' went on Rose; 'she's named Silver, but she's as good as gold. She's a paragon. It's quite a trial to me, rooming with a paragon. But if any more are coming into the entry just give me fair notice, and I pack and move up among the sinners in Attic Row. Somehow, you don't look like paragons either – you especially,' nodding to Clover. 'Your eyes are like violets; but so are Sylvia's – that's my sister – and she's the greatest witch in Massachusetts. Eyes are dreadfully deceitful things. As for you' – to Katy – 'you're so tall that I can't take you all in at once; but the piece I see doesn't look dreadful a bit.'

Rose was sitting in the window as she made these remarks, and, leaning forward suddenly, she gave a pretty, blushing nod to some one below. Katy glanced down, and saw a handsome young man replacing the cap he had lifted from his head.

'That's Berry Searles,' said Rose. 'He's the President's son, you know. He always comes through the side yard to get to his room. That's it – the one with the red curtain.

It's exactly opposite your window. Don't you see?'

'So it is!' exclaimed Katy, remembering what Lilly had said. 'Oh! was that the reason – ' she stopped, afraid of being rude.

'The reason we wanted the room?' inquired Rose, coolly. 'Well, I don't know. It hadn't occurred to me to look at it in that light. Mary,' with sudden severity, 'is it possible that you had Berry Searles in your mind when you were so pertinacious about that room?'

'Rose! How can you? You know I never thought of such a thing,' protested poor Mary.

'I hope not; otherwise I should feel it my duty to consult with Mrs Florence on the subject,' went on Rose, with an air of dignified admonition. 'I consider myself responsible for you and your morals, Mary. Let us change this painful subject.' She looked gravely at the three girls for a moment; then her lips began to twitch, the irresistible dimples appeared in her cheeks, and, throwing herself back in her chair, she burst into a fit of laughter.

'O Mary, you little goose! Some day or other you'll be the death of me! Dear, dear! how I am behaving! It's perfectly horrid of me. And I didn't mean it. I'm going to be real good this term; I promised mother. Please forget it, and don't take a dislike to me, and never come again,' she added, coaxingly, as Katy and Clover rose to go.

'Indeed, we won't,' replied Katy. As for sensible Clover, she was already desperately in love with Rose, on that very first day.

After a couple of hours of hard work, No. 6 was in order, and looked like a different place. Fringed towels were laid over the wash-stand and the table. Dr Carr's photograph and some pretty chromos ornamented the walls; the rocking-chair and the study chair stood by the window; the trunks were hidden by chintz covers, made for the purpose by old Mary. On the window-sill stood Cousin Helen's vase which Katy had brought carefully packed among her clothes. 'Now,' she said, tying the blinds together with a knot of ribbon in imitation of Rose Red's, 'when we get a bunch of wild flowers for my vase, we shall be all right.'

A tap on the door. Rose entered.

'Are you done?' she asked; 'may I come in and see?'

'Oh, this is pretty!' she exclaimed, looking about. 'How you can tell in one minute what sort of girl one is, just by looking at her room! I should know you had been neat and dainty and housekeeperly all your days. And you would see in a minute that I am a Madge Wildfire, and that Ellen Gray is a saint, and Sally Satterlee is a scatterbrain, and Lilly Page an affected little hum – oh, I forgot! she is your cousin, isn't she? How dreadfully rude of me!' dimpling at Clover, who couldn't help dimpling back again.

'Oh, my!' she went on, 'a wash-stand, I declare! Where did you get it?'

'Papa bought it,' explained Katy; 'he asked Mrs Florence's permission.'

'How nice of him! I shall just write to my father to ask for permission too.' Which she did; and the result was that it set the fashion of wash-stands, and so many papas wrote to 'ask permission,' that Mrs Florence found it necessary to give up the lavatory system, and provide wash-stands for the whole house. Katy's request had been the opening wedge. I do not think this fact made her more popular with the principals.

'By the way, where is Lilly?' asked Katy. 'I haven't seen her today.'

'Do you want to know? I can tell you. She's sitting on the edge of one chair, with her feet on the stave of another chair, and her head on the shoulder of her room-mate (who is dying to get away and arrange her drawers); and she's crying –'

'How do you know? Have you been up to see her?'

'Oh! I haven't seen her. It isn't necessary. I saw her last term, and the term before. She always spends the first day at school in that way. I'll take you up, if you'd like to examine for yourselves.'

Katy and Clover, much amused, followed as she led the way upstairs. Sure enough, Lilly was sitting exactly as Rose predicted. Her face was swollen with crying. When she saw the girls, her sobs redoubled.

'Oh! isn't it dreadful?' she demanded. 'I shall die, I know I shall. Oh! why did pa make me come?'

'Now, Lilly, don't be an idiot,' said the unsympathizing Rose. Then she sat down and proceeded to make a series of the most grotesque faces, winking her eyes and twinkling her finger round the head of 'Niobe', as she called Lilly, till the other girls were in fits of laughter, and Niobe, though she shrugged her shoulders pettishly and said, 'Don't be ridiculous, Rose Red,' was forced to give way. First she smiled, then a laugh was heard; afterwards she announced that she felt better.

'That's right, Niobe,' said Rose. 'Wash your face now, and get ready for tea, for the bell is just going to ring. As for you, Annie, you might as well put your drawers

in order,' with a wicked wink. Annie hurried away with
a laugh, which she tried in vain to hide.

'You heartless creature!' cried the exasperated Lilly. 'I
believe you're made of marble; you haven't one bit of
feeling. Nor you either, Katy. You haven't cried a drop.'

'Given this problem,' said the provoking Rose; 'when
the nose without is as red as a lobster, what must be the
temperature of the heart within, and *vice versa*?'

The tea-bell rang just in time to avert a fresh flood of
tears from Lilly. She brushed her hair in angry haste,
and they all hurried down by a side staircase which, as
Rose explained, the school-girls were expected to use.
The dining-room was not large; only part of the girls
could be seated at a time; so they took turns at dining at
the first table, half one week and half the next.

Mrs Nipson sat at the tea-tray, with Mrs Florence
beside her. At the other end of the long board sat a
severe-looking person, whom Lilly announced in a whisper as 'that horrid Miss Jane.' The meal was very simple
– tea, bread and butter, and dried beef: it was eaten in
silence; the girls were not allowed to speak, except to
ask for what they wanted. Rose Red, indeed, who sat
next to Mrs Florence, talked to her, and even ventured
once or twice on daring little jokes, which caused Clover
to regard her with admiring astonishment. No one else
said anything, except, 'Butter, please,' or, 'Pass the
bread.' As they filed upstairs after this cheerless meal,
they were met by rows of hungry girls, who were waiting
to go down, and who whispered, 'How long you have
been! What's for tea?'

The evening passed in making up classes and arranging for recitation-rooms and study-hours. Katy was glad

when bed-time came. The day, with all its new impressions and strange faces, seemed to her like a confused dream. She and Clover undressed very quietly. Among the printed rules, which hung on the bedroom door, they read: 'All communication between roommates, after the retiring-bell has rung, is strictly prohibited.' Just then it did not seem difficult to keep this rule. It was only after the candle was blown out, that Clover ventured to whisper – very low indeed, for who knew but that Miss Jane was listening outside the door? – 'Do you think you're going to like it?' and Katy, in the same cautious whisper, responded, 'I'm not quite sure.' And so ended the first day at the Nunnery.

CHAPTER
5

ROSES AND THORNS

'Oh! What is it? What has happened? cried Clover, starting up in bed, the next morning, as a clanging sound roused her suddenly from sleep. It was only the rising-bell, ringing at the end of Quaker Row.

Katy held her watch up to the dim light. She could just see the hands. Yes, they pointed to six. It was actually morning! She and Clover jumped up, and began to dress as fast as possible.

'We've only got half an hour,' said Clover, unhooking the rules, and carrying them to the window – 'half an hour; and this says we must turn the mattress, smooth the under-sheet over the bolster, and spend five minutes in silent devotion. We'll have to be quick to do all that, besides dressing ourselves!'

It is never easy to be quick, when one is in a hurry. Everything sets itself against you. Fingers turn into thumbs; dresses won't button, nor pins keep their place. With all their haste, Katy and Clover were barely ready when the second bell sounded. As they hastened down-stairs, Katy fastening her breast-pin, and Clover her cuffs, they met other girls, some looking half asleep, others half dressed; all yawning, rubbing their eyes, and complaining of the early hour.

'Isn't it horrid?' said Lilly Page, hurrying by with no collar on, and her hair hastily tucked into a net. 'I never get up till nine o'clock when I'm at home. Ma saves my breakfast for me. She says I shall have my sleep out while I have the chance.

'You don't look quite awake now,' remarked Clover.

'No, because I haven't washed my face. Half the time I don't before breakfast. There's that old mattress has to be turned; and when I sleep too long, I just do that first, and then scramble my clothes on the best way I can. Anything not to be marked!'

After prayers and breakfast were done, the girls had half an hour for putting their bedrooms to rights, during which interval it is to be hoped that Lilly found time to wash her face. After that, lessons began, and lasted till one o'clock. Dinner followed with an hour's 'recreation'; then the bell rang for 'silent study hour', when the girls sat with their books in their bedrooms, but were not allowed to speak to each other. Next came a walk.

'Who are you going to walk with?' asked Rose Red, meeting Clover in Quaker Row.

'I don't know. Katy, I guess.'

'Are you really? You and she like each other, don't you? Do you know, you're the first sisters I ever knew at school who did! Generally, they quarrel awfully. The Stearns girls, who were here last term, scarcely spoke to each other. They didn't even sleep together; and Sarah Stearns was always telling tales against Sue, and Sue against Sarah.'

'How disgusting! I never heard of anything so mean,' cried Clover indignantly. 'Why, I wouldn't tell tales about Katy if we quarrelled ever so much. We never do, though – Katy is so sweet.'

'I suppose she is,' said Rose, rather doubtfully; 'but, do you know, I'm half afraid of her. It's because she's so tall. Tall people always scare me. And then she looks so grave and grown up! Don't tell her I said so though; for I want her to like me.'

'Oh, she isn't a bit grave or grown up. She's the funniest girl in the world. Wait till you know her,' replied loyal Clover.

'I'd give anything if I could walk with you part of this term,' went on Rose, putting her arm round Clover's waist. 'But you see, unluckily, I'm engaged straight through. All of us old girls are. I walk with May Mather this week and next; then Esther Dearborn for a month; then Lilly Page for two weeks; and all the rest of the time with Mary. I can't think why I promised Lilly. I'm sure I don't want to go with her. I'd ask Mary to let me off, only I'm afraid she would not like it. I say, suppose we engage now to walk with each other for the first half of next term.'

'Why, that's not till October!' said Clover.

'I know it; but it's nice to be beforehand. Will you?'

'Of course I will – provided that Katy has somebody pleasant to go with,' replied Clover, immensely flattered at being asked by the popular Rose. Then they ran downstairs, and took their places in the long procession of girls, who were ranged two and two, ready to start. Miss Jane walked at the head; and Miss Marsh, another teacher, brought up the rear. Rose Red whispered that it was like a funeral and a caravan mixed – 'as cheerful as hearses at both ends, and wild beasts in the middle'.

The walk was along a wooded road – a mile out and a mile back. The procession was not permitted to stop, or straggle, or take any of the liberties which make walking pleasant. Still, Katy and Clover enjoyed it. There was a spring smell in the air, and the woods were beginning to be pretty. They even found a little trailing arbutus blossoming in a sunny hollow. Lilly was just in front of them, and amused them with histories of different girls whom she pointed out in the long line. That was Esther Dearborn – Rose Red's friend. Handsome, wasn't she? but terribly sarcastic. The two next were Amy Alsop and Ellen Gray. They always walked together, because they were so intimate. Yes; they were nice enough, only so distressingly good. Amy did not get one single mark last term! That child with pig-tails was Bella Arkwright. Why on earth did Katy want to know about her? She was a nasty little thing.

'She's just about Elsie's height,' replied Katy. 'Who's that pretty girl with pink velvet on her hat?'

'Dear me! Do you think she's pretty? I don't. Her name is Louisa Agnew. She lives at Ashburn – quite near us; but we don't know them. Her family are not at all in good society.'

'What a pity! She looks so sweet and ladylike.'

Lilly tossed her head. 'They're quite common people,' she said. 'They live in a little mite of a house, and her father paints portraits.'

'But I should think that would be nice. Doesn't she ever take you to see his pictures?'

'Take me!' cried Lilly, indignantly. 'I should think not.

I tell you we don't visit. I just speak when we're here, but I never see her when I'm at home.'

'Move on, young ladies. What are you stopping for?' cried Miss Jane.

'Yes; move on,' muttered Rose Red, from behind. 'Don't you hear Policeman X?'

From walking-hour till tea-time was 'recreation' again. Lilly improved this opportunity to call at No. 6. She had waited to see how the girls were likely to take in the school before committing herself to intimacy; but, now that Rose Red had declared in their favour, she was ready to begin to be friendly.

'How lovely!' she said, looking about. 'You got the end room, after all, didn't you? What splendid times you'll have! Oh, how plainly you can see Berry Searles's window! Has he spoken to you yet?'

'Spoken to us? Of course not! Why should he?' replied Katy. 'He doesn't know us, and we don't know him.'

'That's nothing. Half the girls in the school bow, and speak, and carry on with young men they don't know. You won't have a bit of fun if you're so particular.'

'I don't want that kind of fun,' replied Katy, with energy in her voice; 'neither does Clover. And I can't imagine how the girls can behave so. It isn't lady-like at all.'

Katy was very fond of this word, 'lady-like.' She always laid great stress upon it. It seemed in some way to be connected with Cousin Helen, and to mean everything that was good, and graceful, and sweet.

'Dear me! I'd no idea you were so dreadfully proper,' said Lilly, pouting. 'Mother said you were as prim and precise as your grandmother; but I didn't suppose –'

'How unkind!' broke in Clover, taking fire, as usual,

at any affront to Katy. 'Katy prim and precise! She isn't a bit! She's twice as much fun as the rest of you girls; but it's nice fun – not this horrid stuff about students. I wish your mother wouldn't say such things.'

'I didn't – she didn't – I don't mean exactly that,' stammered Lilly, frightened by Clover's indignant eyes. 'All I meant was, that Katy is dreadfully dignified for her age, and we bad girls will have to look out. You needn't be so mad, Clover; I'm sure it's very nice to be proper and good, and set an example.'

'I don't want to preach to anybody,' said Katy, colouring, 'and I wasn't thinking about examples. But really and truly, Lilly, wouldn't your mother, and all the girls' mothers, be shocked if they knew about these performances here?'

'Gracious! I should think so; ma would kill me. I wouldn't have her know of my goings on for all the world.'

Just then Rose pulled out a drawer, and called through to ask if Clover would please come in and help her a minute. Lilly took advantage of her absence to say –

'I came on purpose to ask you to walk with me for four weeks. Will you?'

'Thank you; but I'm engaged to Clover.'

'To Clover! But she's your sister; you can get off.'

'I don't want to get off. Clover and I like dearly to go together.'

Lilly stared. 'Well, I never heard of such a thing,' she said; 'you're really romantic. The girls will call you "The Inseparables".'

'I wouldn't mind being inseparable from Clover,' said Katy.

Next day was Saturday. It was nominally a holiday; but so many tasks were set for it, that it hardly seemed like one. The girls had to practise in the gymnasium, to do their mending, and have all their drawers in apple-pie order, before afternoon, when Miss Jane went through the rooms on a tour of inspection. Saturday, also, was the day for writing home letters; so, altogether, it was about the busiest of the week.

Early in the morning Miss Jane appeared in Quaker Row with some slips of paper in her hand, one of which she left at each door. They told the hours at which the girls were to go to the bath-house.

'You will carry each a bath towel, a sponge, and soap,' she announced to Katy, 'and will be in the entry, at the foot of the stairs, at twenty-five minutes after nine precisely. Failures in punctuality will be punished by a mark.' Miss Jane always delivered her words like a machine, and closed her mouth with a snap at the end of the sentence.

'Horrid thing! Don't I wish her missionary would come and carry her off. Not that I blame him for staying away,' remarked Rose Red, from her door; making a face at Miss Jane as she walked down the entry.

'I don't understand about the bath-house,' said Katy. 'Does it belong to us? And where is it?'

'No, it doesn't belong to us. It belongs to Mr Perrit, and anybody can use it; only on Saturday it is reserved for us nuns. Haven't you ever noticed it when we have been out walking? It's in that street by the bakery, which we pass to take the Lebanon Road. We go across the green, and down by Professor Seccomb's, and we are in plain sight from the college all the way; and, of course, those abominable boys sit there with spy-glasses, and stare as hard as ever they can. It's perfectly horrid. "A bath towel, a sponge, and soap", indeed! I wish I could make Miss Jane eat the pieces of soap which she has forced me to carry across this village.'

'Oh, Rose!' remonstrated Mary Silver.

'Well, I do. And the bath towels afterwards, by way of a dessert,' replied the incorrigible Rose. 'Never mind! Just wait! A bright idea strikes me.'

'Oh! what?' cried the other three; but Rose only pursed up her mouth, arched her eyebrows, and vanished into her own room, locking the door behind her. Mary Silver, finding herself shut out, sat down meekly in the hall till such time as it should please Rose to open the door. This was not till the bath hour. As Katy and Clover went by, Rose put her head out, and called that she would be down in a minute.

The bathing party consisted of eight girls, with Miss Jane for escort. They were half way across the common before Miss Jane noticed that everybody was shaking with stifled laughter, except Rose, who walked along demurely, apparently unconscious that there was anything to laugh at. Miss Jane looked sharply from one to another for a moment, then stopped short and exclaimed, 'Rosamund Redding! how dare you?'

'What is it, ma'am?' asked Rose, with the face of a lamb.

'Your bath towel! your sponge!' gasped Miss Jane.

'Yes, ma'am, I have them all,' replied the audacious Rose, putting her hand to her hat. There, to be sure, was the long towel, hanging down behind like a veil, while the sponge was fastened on one side like a great cockade; and in front appeared a cake of pink soap, neatly pinned into the middle of a black velvet bow.

Miss Jane seized Rose and removed these ornaments in a twinkling. 'We shall see what Mrs Florence thinks of this conduct,' she grimly remarked. Then, dropping the soap and sponge in her own pocket, she made Rose walk beside her, as if she were a criminal in custody.

The bath-house was a neat place, with eight small rooms, well supplied with hot and cold water. Katy would have found her bath very nice, had it not been for the thought of the walk home. They must look so absurd with their sponges and damp towels.

Miss Jane was as good as her word. After dinner, Rose was sent for by Mrs Florence, and had an interview of two hours with her; she came out with red eyes, and shut herself into her room with a disconsolate bang. Before long, however, she revived sufficiently to tap on the drawers and push through a note with the following words:

> My heart is broken!
> R.R.

Clover hastened in to comfort her. Rose was sitting on the floor, with a very clean pocket-handkerchief in her hand. She wept, and put her head against Clover's knee.

'I suppose I'm the nastiest girl in the world,' she said. 'Mrs Florence thinks so. She said I was an evil influence in the school. Wasn't that unkind?' with a little sob.

'I meant to be so good this term,' she went on; 'but what's the use? A codfish might as well try to play the piano! It was always so, even when I was a baby. Sylvia says I have got a little fiend inside of me. Do you believe I have? Is it that makes me so horrid?'

Clover purred over her. She could not bear to have Rose feel unhappy. 'Wasn't Miss Jane funny?' went on Rose, with a sudden twinkle; 'and did you see Berry, and Alfred Seccomb?'

'No; where were they?'

'Close to us, standing by the fence. All the time Miss Jane was unpinning the towel, they were splitting their sides, and Berry made such a face at me that I nearly laughed out. That boy has a perfect genius for faces. He used to frighten Sylvia and me into fits, when we were little tots, up here on visits.'

'Then you knew him before you came to school?'

'Oh dear, yes! I know all the Hillsover boys. We used to make mud pies together. They're grown up now, most of them, and in college; and when we meet we're very dignified, and say, "Miss Redding", and "Mr Seccomb", and "Mr Searles"; but we're just as good friends as ever. When I go to take tea with Mrs Seccomb, Alfred always invites Berry to drop in, and we have the greatest fun. Mrs Florence won't let me go this term, though, I guess, she's so mad about the towel.'

Katy was quite relieved when Clover reported this conversation. Rose, for all her wickedness, seemed to be a little lady. Katy did not like to class her among the girls who flirted with students whom they did not know.

It was wonderful how soon they all settled down, and became accustomed to their new life. Before six weeks were over, Katy and Clover felt as if they had lived at Hillsover for years. This was partly because there was so much to do. Nothing makes time fly like having every moment filled, and every hour set apart for a distinct employment.

They made several friends, chief among whom were Ellen Gray and Louisa Agnew; this last intimacy Lilly resented highly, and seemed to consider as an affront to herself. With no one, however, was Katy so intimate as Clover was with Rose Red. This cost Katy some jealous pangs at first. She was so used to considering Clover her own exclusive property that it was not easy to share her with another; and she had occasional fits of feeling resentful and injured, and left out. These were but momentary, however. Katy was too good of heart to let unkind feelings grow, and by and by she grew fond of Rose and Rose of her, so that in the end the sisters shared their friend as they did other nice things, and neither of them was jealous of the other.

But, charming as she was, a certain price had to be paid for the pleasure of intimacy with Rose. Her overflowing spirits, and 'the little fiend inside her', were always provoking scrapes in which her friends were apt to be more or less involved. She was very penitent and afflicted after these scrapes, but it didn't make a bit of difference; the next time she was just as naughty as ever.

'What are you doing?' said Katy one day, meeting her in the hall with a heap of black shawls and aprons on her arm.

'Hush!' whispered Rose, mysteriously; 'don't say a word. Senator Brown is dead – our senator, you know. I'm going to put my window into mourning for him, that's all. It's a proper token of respect.'

Two hours later, Mrs Nipson, walking sedately across the common, noticed quite a group of students in the

President's side yard, looking up at the Nunnery. She drew nearer. They were admiring Rose's window, hung with black, and decorated with a photograph of the deceased senator, suspended in the middle of a wreath of weeping-willow. Of course she hurried upstairs, and tore down the shawls and aprons; and, equally of course, Rose had a lecture and a mark. But, dear me! what good did it do? The next day but one, as Katy and Clover sat together in silent-study hour, their lower drawer was pushed open very noiselessly and gently, till it came out entirely, and lay on the floor, and in the aperture thus formed appeared Rose's saucy face, flushed with mischief. She was crawling through from her own room.

'Such fun!' she whispered; 'I never thought of this before! We can have parties in study hours, and all sorts of things.'

'Oh, go back, Rosy!' whispered Clover, in agonized entreaty, though laughing all the time.

'Go back? Not at all! I'm coming in,' answered Rose, pulling herself through a little farther. But at that moment the door opened: there stood Miss Jane! She had caught the buzz of voices as she passed in the hall, and had entered to see what was going on.

Rose, dreadfully frightened, made a rapid movement to withdraw. But the space was narrow, and she had wedged herself, and could move neither backward nor forward. She had to submit to being helped through by Miss Jane, in a series of pulls, while Katy and Clover sat by, not daring to laugh or offer assistance. When Rose was on her feet, Miss Jane released her with a final shake, which she seemed unable to refrain from giving.

'Go to your room,' she said. 'I shall report all of

you young ladies for this flagrant act of disobedience.'

Rose went, and in two minutes the drawer, which Miss Jane had replaced, opened again, and there was this note:

> If I am never heard of more, give my love to my family, and mention how I died. I forgive my enemies, and leave Clover my band bracelet.
>
> My blessings on you both.
>
> > With the deepest regard,
> >
> > > Your afflicted friend,
> > >
> > > > R.R.

Mrs Florence was very angry on this occasion, and would listen to no explanations, but gave Katy and Clover a 'disobedience mark' also. This was very unfair, and Rose felt dreadfully about it. She begged and entreated, but Mrs Florence only replied, 'There is blame on both sides, I have no doubt.'

'She's entirely changed from what she used to be,' declared Rose. 'I don't know what's the matter; I don't like her half so much as I did.'

The truth was, that Mrs Florence had secretly determined to give up her connection with the school at Midsummer; and, regarding it now rather as Mrs Nipson's school than her own, she took no pains to study character or mete out justice carefully among scholars with whom she was not likely to have much to do.

CHAPTER
6

THE S.S.U.C.

It was Saturday afternoon, and Clover, having finished her practising, dusting, and mending, had settled herself in No. 6 for a couple of hours of quiet enjoyment. Everything was in beautiful order to meet Miss Jane's inspecting eye; and Clover, as she sat in the rocking-chair, writing-case in lap, looked extremely cosy and comfortable.

A half-finished letter to Elsie lay in the writing-case; but Clover felt lazy, and instead of writing was looking out of the window, in a dreamy way, to where Berry Searles and some other young men were playing ball in the yard below. She was not thinking of them or of anything else in particular. A vague sense of pleasant idleness possessed her, and it was like the breaking of a dream when the door opened and Katy came in, not quietly, after her wont, but with a certain haste and indignant rustle, as if vexed by something. When she saw Clover at the window she cried out hastily, 'Oh, Clover, don't!'

'Don't what?' asked Clover, without turning her head.

'Don't sit there looking at those boys.'

'Why? why not? They can't see me. The blinds are shut.'

'No matter for that. It's just as bad as if they could see you. Don't do it. I would much rather that you did not.'

'Well, I won't then,' said Clover, good-humouredly, facing round with her back to the window. 'I wasn't looking at them either – not exactly. I was thinking about Elsie and John, and wondering – But what's the matter, Katy? What makes you fire up so about it? You've watched the ball-playing yourself, plenty of times.'

'I know I have, and I didn't mean to be cross, Clover. The truth is, I am very much put out. These girls, with their incessant talk about the students, make me absolutely sick. It is so unlady-like and so bad, especially for the little ones. Fancy that mite of a Carrie Steele informing me that she is "in love" with Harry Crosby. In love! A baby like that! She has no business to know that there is such a thing.'

'Yes,' said Clover, laughing; 'she wrote his name on a winter-green lozenge, and bored a hole and hung it round her neck on a blue ribbon. But it melted and stuck to her frock, and she had to take it off.'

'Whereupon she ate it,' added Rose, who came in at that moment. The girls shouted, but Katy soon grew grave. 'One can't help laughing,' she said; 'but isn't it a shame to have such things going on? Just fancy our Elsie behaving so, Clover! Why, papa would have a fit. I declare I've a great mind to get up a society to put down flirting.'

'Do,' said Rose. 'What fun it would be! Call it "The Society for the Suppression of Young Men". I'll join.'

'You, indeed!' replied Katy, shaking her head. 'Didn't I see Berry Searles throw a bunch of syringa into your window only this morning?'

'Dear me! did he? I shall have to speak to Mary again. It's quite shocking to have her go on so. But really and truly do let us have a Society. It would be so jolly. We could meet on Saturday afternoons, and write pieces and have signals and a secret, as Sylvia's Society did when she was at school. Get one up, Katy – that's a dear.'

'But,' said Katy, taken aback by having her random idea so suddenly adopted, 'if I did get one up, it would be in real earnest, and it would be a society against flirting. And you know you can't help it, Rosy.'

'Yes, I can. You are doing me great injustice. I don't behave like those girls in Attic Row. I never did. I just bow to Berry and the rest whom I really know – never to anybody else. And you must see, Katherine darling, that it would be the height of ingratitude if I didn't bow to boys who made mud pies for me when I was little, and lent me their marbles, and did all sorts of kind things. Now wouldn't it?' – coaxingly.

'Per – haps,' admitted Katy, with a smile. 'But you're such a witch!'

'I'm not – indeed I'm not. I'll be a pillar of society if only you'll provide a society for me to be a pillar of. Now, Katy, do – ah, do, do!'

When Rose was in a coaxing mood, few people could resist her. Katy yielded, and between jest and earnest the matter was settled. Katy was to head the plan and invite the members.

'Only a few at first,' suggested Rose. 'When it is proved to be a success, and everybody wants to join, we can let in two or three more as a great favour. What shall the name be? We'll keep it a secret, whatever it is. There's no fun in a society without a secret.'

What should the name be? Rose invented half a dozen, each more absurd than the last. 'The Anti-Jane Society' would sound well, she insisted. Or, no! the 'Put-him-down Club' was better yet! Finally they settled upon 'The Society for the Suppression of Unladylike Conduct'.

'Only we'll never use the whole name,' said Rose; 'we'll say, "The S. S. U. C." That sounds brisk and snappy, and will drive the whole school wild with curiosity. What larks! How I long to begin!'

The next Saturday was fixed upon for the first meeting. During the week Katy proposed the plan to the elect few.

Lilly Page was the only person who declined. She said it would be stupid; that for her part she didn't set up to be good or better than she was, and that in any case she shouldn't wish to be mixed up in a society of which 'Miss Agnew' was a member. The girls did not break their hearts over this refusal. They had felt obliged to ask her for relationship's sake, but everybody was a little relieved that she did not wish to join.

No. 6 looked very full indeed that Saturday afternoon when the S. S. U. C. came together for the first time. Ten members were present. Mary Silver and Louisa were two; and Rose's crony, Esther Dearborn, another. The remaining four were Sally Alsop and Amy Erskine; Alice Gibbons, one of the new scholars, whom they all liked, but did not know very well; and Ellen Gray, a pale, quiet girl, with droll blue eyes, a comical twist to her mouth, and a trick of saying funny things in such a demure way that half the people who listened never found out that they were funny. All Rose's chairs had been borrowed for the occasion. Three girls sat on the bed, and three on the floor. With a little squeezing, there was plenty of room for everybody.

Katy was chosen President, and requested to take the rocking-chair as a sign of office. This she did with much dignity, and proceeded to read the Constitution and Bye-Laws of the Society, which had been drawn up by Rose Red, and copied on an immense sheet of blue paper.

They ran thus:

CONSTITUTION OF THE SOCIETY FOR THE SUPPRESSION OF UNLADYLIKE CONDUCT, KNOWN TO THE UNINITIATED AS THE S.S.U.C.

Article I

The object of this Society is two-fold: it combines having a good time with the pursuit of VIRTUE.

Article II

The good time is to take place once a week in No. 6, Quaker Row, between the hours of four and six p.m.

Article III

The nature of the good time is to be decided upon by a Committee to be appointed each Saturday by the members of the Society.

Article IV

VIRTUE is to be pursued at all times and in all seasons, by the members of the Society setting their faces against – 'The window-panes,' put in Red Rose – 'No, the practice of bowing and speaking to College students who are not acquaintances,' read on Katy, shaking her head at naughty Rose – 'waving handkerchiefs, signals from windows, and every species of unladylike conduct.'

Article V

The members of the Society pledge themselves to use their influence against these practices, both by precept and example.

In witness whereof we sign,

Katherine Carr, *President*.
Rosamund Redding, *Secretary*.
Clover E. Carr.
Mary L. Silver.

Esther Dearborn.
Sally P. Alsop.
Amy W. Erskine.
Alice Gibbons.
Ellen Whitworth Gray.

Next followed the Bye-Laws. Katy had not been able to see the necessity of having any Bye-Laws, but Rose had insisted. She had never heard of a Society without them, she said, and she didn't think it would be 'legal' to leave them out. It had cost her some trouble to invent them, but at last they stood thus:

Bye-Law No. 1

The members of the S.S.U.C. will observe the following signals:
    1st. *The Grip* – This is given by inserting the first and middle finger of the right hand between the thumb and fourth finger of the respondent's left, and describing a rotatory motion in the air with the little finger. N.B. – Much practice is necessary

to enable members to exchange this signal in such a manner as not to attract attention.

2nd. *The Signal of Danger* – This signal is for use when Miss Jane, or any other foe-woman, heaves in sight. It consists in rubbing the nose violently, and at the same time giving three stamps on the floor with the left foot. It must be done with an air of unconsciousness.

3rd. *The Signal for Consultation* – This signal is for use when immediate communication is requisite between members of the Society. It consists of a pinch on the back of the right hand, accompanied by the word 'Holofernes' pronounced in a low voice.

Bye-Law No. 2

The members of the S.S.U.C. pledge themselves to inviolable secrecy about all Society proceedings.

Bye-Law No. 3

The members of the S.S.U.C. will bring their Saturday corn-balls to swell the common entertainment.

Bye-Law No. 4

Members having boxes from home are at liberty to contribute such part of the contents as they please to the aforementioned common entertainment.

Here the Bye-Laws ended. There was much laughter over them, especially over the last.

'Why did you put that in, Rosy?' asked Ellen Gray; 'it strikes me as hardly necessary.'

'Oh,' replied Rose, 'I put that in to encourage Silvery Mary there! She's expecting a box soon, and I knew that she would pine to give the Society a share, but would be too timid to propose it; so I thought I would just pave the way.'

'How truly kind!' laughed Clover.

'Now,' said the President, 'the entertainment of the meeting will begin by the reading of "Trailing Arbutus", a poem by C. E. C.'

Clover had been very unwilling to read the first piece, and had only yielded after much coaxing from Rose, who had bestowed upon her in consequence the name of Quintia Curtia. She felt very shy as she stood up with her paper in her hand, and her voice trembled perceptibly; but after a minute she grew used to the sound of it, and read steadily.

TRAILING ARBUTUS
I always think, when looking
    At its mingled rose and white,
Of the pink lips of children
    Put up to say good-night.

Cuddled its green leaves under,
    Like babies in their beds,
Its blossoms shy and sunny
    Conceal their pretty heads

And when I lift the blanket up,
    And peep inside of it,
They seem to give me smile for smile,
    Nor be afraid a bit.

Dear little flower, the earliest
    Of all the flowers that are!
Twinkling upon the bare, brown earth
    As on the clouds a star.

How can we fail to love it well,
    Or prize it more and more!
It is the first small signal
    That winter time is o'er!

> That Spring has not forgotten us,
>   Though late and slow she be,
> But is upon her flying way,
>   And we her face shall see.

This production caused quite a sensation among the girls. They had never heard any of Clover's verses before, and thought these wonderful.

'Why,' cried Sally Alsop, 'it is almost as good as Tupper!'

Sally meant this for a great compliment, for she was devoted to the 'Proverbial Philosophy'.

'A Poem by E. D.' was the next thing on the list. Esther Dearborn rose with great pomp and dignity, cleared her throat, put on a pair of eyeglasses, and began –

MISS JANE

> Who ran to catch me on the spot
> If I the slightest rule forgot,
> Believing and excusing not?
>
> Miss Jane.

> Who lurked outside my door all day,
> In hopes that I would disobey,
> And some low whispered word would say?
>
> Miss Jane.

> Who sternly bade me come and go,
> Do this, do that, or else forego
> The other thing I longed for so?
>
> Miss Jane.

> Who caught our Rose-bud half-way through
> The wall which parted her from two
> Friends, and that small prank made her rue?
>
> Miss Jane.

Who is our bane, our foe, our fear?
Who's always certain to appear
Just when we do not think her near?

Miss Jane.

'Who down the hall is creeping now
With stealthy step, but knowing not how
Exactly to discover – '

broke in Rose, improvising rapidly. Next moment came
a knock at the door. It was Miss Jane.

'Your drawers, Miss Carr – your cupboard,' she said,
going across the room, and examining each in turn.
There was no fault to be found with either, so she
withdrew, giving the laughing girls a suspicious glance,
and remarking that it was a bad habit to sit on beds – it
always injured them.

'Do you suppose she heard?' whispered Mary Silver.

'No, I don't think she did,' replied Rose. 'Of course
she suspected us of being in some mischief or other –
she always does that. Now, Mary, it's your turn to give
us an intellectual treat. Begin.'

Poor Mary shrank back, blushing and protesting.

'You know I can't,' she said, 'I'm too stupid.'

'Rubbish!' cried Rose. 'You're the dearest girl that ever
was.' She gave Mary's shoulder a reassuring pat.

'Mary is excused this time,' put in Katy. 'It is the first
meeting, so I shall be indulgent. But, after this, every
member will be expected to contribute something for
each meeting. I mean to be very strict.'

'Oh, I never, never can!' cried Mary.

Rose was down on her at once.

'Nonsense! hush!' she said. 'Of course you can. You shall, if I have to write it for you myself.'

'Order!' said the President, rapping on the table with a pencil. 'Rose has something to read to us.'

Rose stood up with great gravity. 'I would ask for a moment's delay, that the Society may get out its pocket-handkerchiefs,' she said. 'My piece is an affecting one. I didn't mean it, but it came so. We cannot always be cheerful.' Here she heaved a sigh, which set the S.S.U.C. to laughing, and began –

A SCOTCH POEM
Wee, crimson-tipped Willie Wink,
   Wae's me, drear, dree, and dra,
A waeful thocht, a fearsome flea,
   A wuthering wind, an a'.

Sair, sair thy mither sabs her lane,
   He een, her mou, are wat;

Her cauld kail hae the corbie ta'en,
   And grierously she grat.

Ah, me, the suthering of the wind!
   Ah, me, the waesome mither!
Ah, me, the bairnies left ahind,
   The shither, hither, blither!

'What *does* it mean?' cried the girls, as Rose folded up the paper and sat down.

'Mean?' said Rose; 'I'm sure I don't know, it's Scotch, I tell you. It's the kind of thing that people read, and then they say. "One of the loveliest gems that Burns ever wrote!" I thought I'd see if I couldn't do one too. Anybody can, I find; it's not at all difficult.'

All the poems having been read, Katy now proposed that they should play 'Word and Question'. She and Clover were accustomed to the game at home, but to some of the others it was quite new.

Each girl was furnished with a slip of paper and a pencil, and was told to write a word at the top of the paper, fold it over, and pass it to her next left-hand neighbour.

'Dear me! I don't know what to write,' said Mary Silver.

'Oh, write anything!' said Clover.

So Mary obediently wrote 'Anything,' and folded it over.

'What next?' asked Alice Gibbons.

'Now a question,' said Katy. 'Write it under the word, and fold over again. No, Amy, not on the fold. Don't you see, if you do, the writing will be on the wrong side of the paper when we come to read?'

The questions were more troublesome than the words, and the girls sat frowning and biting their pencil-tops for some minutes before all were done. As the slips were handed in, Katy dropped them into the lid of her work-basket, and thoroughly mixed and stirred them.

'Now,' she said, passing it about, 'each one draw one, read, and write a rhyme in which the word is introduced and the question answered. It needn't be more than two lines, unless you like. Here, Rose, it's your turn first!'

'Oh, what a hard game!' cried some of the girls; but pretty soon they grew interested, and began to work over their verses.

'I should uncommonly like to know who wrote this

abominable word,' said Rose, in a tone of despair. 'Clover, you witch, I believe it was you.'

Clover peeped over her shoulder, nodded, and laughed.

'Very well, then!' snatching up Clover's slip, and putting her own in its place, 'you can just write on it yourself – I shan't! I never heard of such a word in my life! You made it up for the occasion, you know you did!'

'I didn't! it's in the Bible,' replied Clover, setting to work composedly on the fresh paper.

But when Rose opened Clover's slip, she groaned again.

'It's just as bad as the other,' she cried. 'Do change back again, Clovy, that's a dear.'

'No, indeed!' said Clover, guarding her paper; 'you've changed once, and now you must keep what you have.'

Rose made a face, chewed her pencil awhile, and then began to write rapidly. For some minutes not a word was spoken.

'I've done,' said Esther Dearborn at last, flinging her paper into the basket-lid.

'So have I,' said Katy.

One by one the papers were collected and jumbled into a heap. Then Katy, giving all a final shake, drew out one, opened it, and read.

Word – Radishes.

Question – How do you like your clergymen done?
How do I like them done? Well, that depends.
I like them *done* on sleepy, drowsy Sundays!
I like them under-done on other days!

> Perhaps a little *over*-done on Mondays,
> But always I prefer them old as pa.
> And not like radishes, all red and raw.

'Oh, *what* a rhyme!' cried Clover.

'Well, what is one to do?' said Ellen Gray. Then she stopped and bit her lip, remembering that no one was supposed to know who wrote the separate papers.

'Aha! it's yours, is it, Ellen?' said Rose. 'You're an awfully clever girl, and an ornament to the S.S.U.C. Go on, Katy.'

Katy opened the second slip.

Word – Anything.

Question – Would you rather be a greater fool than you seem, or seem a greater fool than you are?

> I wouldn't seem a fool for anything, my dear,
> If I could help it; but I can't, I fear.

'Not bad,' said Rose, nodding her head at Sally Alsop, who blushed crimson.

The third paper ran –

Word – Mahershahalhashbaz.

Question – Does your mother know you're out?

Rose and Clover exchanged looks.

> Why, of course my mother knows it,
>   For she sent me out herself, and
> She told me to run quickly, for
>   It wasn't but a mile;
> But I found it was much farther
>   And my feet grew tired and weary,

And I couldn't hurry greatly,
   So it took a long, long while.
Beside, I stopped to read your word,
   A stranger one I never heard!
I've met with *Pa*-pistical,
         That's pat;
But *Ma*-hershahalhashbaz,
         What's that?

'Oh, Clovy, you bright little thing!' cried Rose, in fits of laughter.

But Mary Silver looked quite pale.

'I never heard of anything so awful!' she said. 'If that word had come to me, I should have fainted away on the spot – I know I should!'

Next came –

Word – Buttons.

Question – What is the best way to make home happy?

To me 'tis quite clear I can answer this right:
Sew on the buttons, and sew them on tight.

'I suspect that is Amy's,' said Esther; 'she's such a model for mending and keeping things in order.'

'It's not fair guessing aloud in this way,' said Sally Alsop. Sally always spoke for Amy, and Amy for Sally. 'Voice and Echo' Rose called them; only, as she remarked, nobody could tell which was Echo and which Voice.

The next word was 'Mrs Nipson', and the question, 'Do you like flowers?'

Do I like flowers? I will not write a sonnet,
   Singing their beauty as a poet might do:

> I just detest those on Aunt Nipson's bonnet,
> > Because they're just like her – all grey and blue,
> > Dusty and pinched, and fastened on askew!
> And as for heaven's own buttercups and daisies,
> I am not good enough to sing their praises.

Nobody knew who wrote this verse. Katy suspected Louisa, and Rose suspected Katy.

The sixth slip was a very brief one.

Word – When?

Question – Are you willing?

> > If I wasn't willing, I would tell you;
> > But when – Oh, dear, I *can't.*

'What an extraordinary rhyme!' began Clover; but Rose spied poor Mary blushing and looking distressed, and hastily interposed –

'It's very good, I'm sure. I wish I'd written it. Go on, Katy.'

So Katy went on.

Word – Unfeeling.

Question – Which would you rather, do, or go fishing?

> > I don't feel up to fishing, or sich;
> > And so, if you please, I'd rather do – which?

'I don't seem to see the word in that poem,' said Rose. 'The distinguished author will please write another.'

'The distinguished author' made no reply to this suggestion; but, after a minute or two, Esther Dearborn, 'quite disinterestedly', as she stated, remarked that, after all, to 'don't feel' was pretty much the same as unfeeling.

There was a little chorus of groans at this, and Katy said she should certainly impose a fine if such dodges and evasions were practised again. This was the first meeting, however, and she would be merciful. After this speech she unfolded another paper. It ran –

Word – Flea.

Question – What would you do, love?

What would I do, love? Well, I do not know.
How can I tell till you are more explicit?
If 'twere a rose you held me, I would smell it;
If 'twere a mouth you held me, I would kiss it;
If 'twere a frog, I'd scream than furies louder;
If 'twere a flea, I'd fetch the Lyon's powder.

Only two slips remained. One was Katy's own. She knew it by the way in which it was folded, and had almost instinctively avoided and left it for the last. Now, however, she took courage and opened it. The word was 'Measles', and the question, 'Who was the grandmother of Invention?' These were the lines:

The night it was horribly dark,
The measles broke out in the Ark:
Little Japhet, and Shem, and all the young Hams,
Were screaming at once for potatoes and clams.
And 'What shall I do,' said poor Mrs Noah,
'And alone by myself in this terrible shower?
I know what I'll do: I'll step down in the hold,
And wake up a lioness grim and old,
And tie her close to the children's door,
And give her a ginger-cake to roar
At the top of her voice for an hour or more;
And I'll tell the children to cease their din,

Or I'll let that grim old party in,
To stop their squeazles and likewise their measles.' –
She practised this with the greatest success.
She was every one's grandmother, I guess.

'That's much the best of all!' pronounced Alice Gibbons.
'I wonder who wrote it?'

'Dear me! did you like it so much?' said Rose, simpering, and doing her best to blush.

'Did you really write it?' said Mary; but Louisa laughed, and exclaimed, 'No use, Rosy! you can't take us in – we know better!'

'Now for the last,' said Katy. 'The word is 'Buckwheat', and the question, 'What is the origin of dreams?'

When the nuns are sweetly sleeping,
Mrs Nipson comes a-creeping,
Creeping like a kitty-cat from door to door;
And she listens to their slumbers,
And most carefully she numbers,
Counting for every nun a nunlet snore!
And the nuns in sweet forgetfulness who lie,
Dreaming of buckwheat cakes, parental love, and – pie,
Moan softly, twist and turn, and see
Black cats and fiends, who frolic in their glee;
And nightmares prancing wildly do abound
While Mrs Nipson makes her nightly round.

'Who did write that?' exclaimed Rose. Nobody answered. The girls looked at each other, and Rose scrutinized them all with sharp glances.

'Well! I never saw such creatures for keeping their countenances,' she said. 'Somebody is as bold as brass. Didn't you see how I blushed when my piece was read?'

'You monkey!' whispered Clover, who at that moment caught sight of the handwriting on the paper. Rose gave her a warning pinch, and they both subsided with an unseen giggle.

'What! The tea-bell!' cried everybody. 'We wanted to play another game.'

'It's a complete success!' whispered Rose, ecstatically, as they went down the hall. 'The girls all say they never had such fun in their lives. I'm so glad I didn't die with the measles when I was little!'

'Well,' demanded Lilly, 'so the high and mighty Society has had a meeting! How did it go off?'

'*De*licious!' replied Rose, smacking her lips as at the recollection of something very nice. 'But you mustn't ask any questions, Lilly. Outsiders have nothing to do with the S.S.U.C. Our proceedings are strictly private.' She ran downstairs with Katy.

'I think you're real mean!' called Lilly after them. Then she said to herself, 'They're just trying to tease. I know it was stupid.'

CHAPTER

7

INJUSTICE

Summer was always slow in getting to Hillsover, but at last she arrived, and woods and hills suddenly put on new colours and became beautiful. The sober village shared in the glorifying process. Vines budded on piazzas. Wisteria purpled whitewashed wall. The brown elm boughs which hung above the common turned into trailing garlands of fresh green. Each walk revealed some change, or ended in some delightful discovery, trilliums, dog-tooth violets, apple-trees in blossom, or wild strawberries turning red. The wood flowers and mosses, even the birds and bird-songs, were new to our Western girls. Hillsover, in summer, was a great deal prettier than Burnet, and Katy and Clover began to enjoy school very much indeed.

Towards the end of June, however, something took place which gave them quite a different feeling – something so disagreeable that I hate to tell about it; but, as it really happened, I must.

It was on a Saturday morning. They had just come back from the bath-house, and were going upstairs, laughing, and feeling very merry; for Clover had written a droll piece for the S.S.U.C. meeting, and was telling Katy about it, when, just at the head of the stairs, they met Rose Red. She was evidently in trouble, for she looked flushed and excited, and was under the escort of Miss Barnes, who marched before her with the air of a policeman. As she passed the girls, Rose opened her eyes very wide, and made a face expressive of dismay.

'What's the matter?' whispered Clover. Rose only made another grimace, clawed with her fingers at Miss Barnes' back, and vanished down the entry which led to Mrs Florence's room. They stood looking after her.

'Oh dear!' sighed Clover, 'I'm so afraid Rose is in a scrape.'

They walked on towards Quaker Row. In the washroom was a knot of girls, with their heads close together, whispering. When they saw Katy and Clover, they became silent, and gazed at them curiously.

'What has Rose Red gone to Mrs Florence about?' asked Clover, too anxious to notice the strange manner of the girls. But at that moment she caught sight of something which so amazed her that she forgot her question. It was nothing less than her own trunk, with 'C. E. C.' at the end, being carried along the entry by two men. Miss Jane followed close behind, with her arms full of clothes and books. Katy's well-known scarlet pincushion topped the pile; in Miss Jane's hand were Clover's comb and brush.

'Why, what does this mean?' gasped Clover, as she and Katy darted after Miss Jane, who had turned into one of the rooms. It was No. 1, at the head of the row – a room which no one had wanted, on account of its smallness and lack of light. The window looked out on a brick wall not ten feet away; there was never a ray of sun to make it cheerful; and Mrs Nipson had converted it into a store-room for empty trunks. The trunks were taken away now, and the bed was strewn with Katy's and Clover's possessions.

'Miss Jane, what is the matter? What are you moving our things for?' exclaimed the girls in great excitement.

Miss Jane laid down her load of dresses, and looked at them sternly.

'You know the reason as well as I do,' she said icily.

'No, I don't. I haven't the least idea what you mean!' cried Katy. 'Oh, please be careful!' as Miss Jane flung a pair of boots on top of Cousin Helen's vase, 'you'll break it! Dear, dear! Clover, there's your Cologne bottle tipped over, and all the Cologne spilt! What does it mean? Is our room going to be painted, or what?'

'Your room,' responded Miss Jane, 'is for the future to be this – No. 1. Miss Benson and Miss James will take No. 6; and, it is to be hoped, will conduct themselves more properly than you have done.'

'Than we have done!' cried Katy, hardly believing her ears.

'Do not repeat my words in that rude way!' said Miss Jane, tartly. 'Yes, than you have done!'

'But what have we done? There is some dreadful mistake! Do tell us what you mean, Miss Jane! We have done nothing wrong, so far as I know.'

'Indeed!' replied Miss Jane, sarcastically. 'Your ideas of right and wrong must be peculiar! I advise you to say no more on the subject, but be thankful that Mrs Florence keeps you in the school at all, instead of dismissing you.

Nothing but the fact that your home is at such a distance prevents her from doing so.'

Katy felt as if all the blood in her body were turned to fire as she heard these words, and met Miss Jane's eyes. Her old, hasty temper, which had seemed to die out during years of pain and patience, flashed into sudden life, as a smouldering coal flashes, when you least expect it, into flame. She drew herself up to her full height, gave Miss Jane a look of scorching indignation, and, with a rapid impulse, darted out of the room and along the hall towards Mrs Florence's door. The girls she met scattered from her path right and left. She looked so tall and moved so impetuously that she absolutely frightened them.

'Come in,' said Mrs Florence, in answer to her sharp, quivering knock. Katy entered. Rose was not there, and Mrs Florence and Mrs Nipson sat together, side by side, in close consultation.

'Mrs Florence,' said Katy, too much excited to feel in the least afraid, 'will you please tell me why our things are being changed to No. 1?'

Mrs Florence flushed with anger. She looked Katy all over for a minute before she answered; then she said, in a severe voice, 'It is done by my orders, and for good and sufficient reasons. What those reasons are, you know as well as I.'

'No, I do not!' replied Katy, as angry as Mrs Florence. 'I have not the least idea what they are, and I insist on knowing!'

'I cannot answer questions put in such an improper manner,' said Mrs Florence, with a wave of the hand, which meant that Katy was to go, but Katy did not stir.

'I am sorry if my manner was improper,' she said, trying to speak quietly, 'but I think I have a right to ask what this means. If we are accused of doing wrong, it is only fair to tell us what it is.'

Mrs Florence only waved her hand again; but Mrs Nipson, who had been twisting uneasily in her chair, said, 'Excuse me, Mrs Florence, but perhaps it would be better – would satisfy Miss Carr better – if you were to be explicit.'

'It does not seem to me that Miss Carr can be in need of any explanation,' replied Mrs Florence. 'When a young lady writes under-hand notes to young gentlemen, and throws them from her window, and they are discovered, she must naturally expect that persons of correct ideas will be shocked and disgusted. Your note to Mr Abernethy Searles, Miss Carr, was found by his mother while mending his pocket, and was handed by her to me. After this statement, you will hardly be surprised that I do not consider it best to permit you to room longer on that side of the house. I did not suppose I had a girl in my school capable of such conduct.'

For a moment Katy was too much stunned to speak. She took hold of a chair to steady herself, and her colour changed so quickly from red to pale and back again to red, that Mrs Florence and Mrs Nipson, who sat watching her, might be pardoned for thinking that she looked guilty. As soon as she recovered her voice, she stammered out, 'But I didn't! I never did! I haven't written any note! I wouldn't for the world! Oh, Mrs Florence, please believe me!'

'I prefer to believe the evidence of my eyes,' replied Mrs Florence, as she drew a paper from her pocket.

'Here is the note. I suppose you will hardly deny your own signature.'

Katy seized the note. It was written in a round, unformed hand, and ran thus:

DEAR BERRY,

'I saw you last night on the Green. I think you are splendid. All the nuns think so. I look at you very often out of my window. If I let down a string, would you tie a cake to it, like that kind which you threw to Mary Andrews last term? Tie two cakes, please; one for me, and one for my room-mate. The string will be at the end of the Row.

MISS CARR

In spite of her agitation, Katy could hardly keep back a smile as she read this absurd production. Mrs Florence saw the smile, and her tone was more severe than ever, as she said –

'Give that back to me, if you please. It will be my justification with your father if he objects to your change of room.'

'But, Mrs Florence,' cried Katy, 'I never wrote that note. It isn't my handwriting; it isn't my – Oh, surely, you can't think so! It's too ridiculous.'

'Go to your room at once,' said Mrs Florence, 'and be thankful that your punishment is such a mild one. If your home were not so distant, I should write to ask your father to remove you from the school; instead of which, I merely put you on the side of the entry, out of reach of further correspondence of this sort.'

'But I shall write him, and he will take us away immediately,' cried Katy, stung to the quick by this obstinate injustice. 'I will not stay, neither shall Clover, where our

word is disbelieved, and we are treated like this. Papa
knows! Papa will never doubt us a moment when we
tell him that this is not true.'

With these passionate words she left the room. I do
not think that either Mrs Florence or Mrs Nipson felt
very comfortable after she was gone.

That was a dreadful afternoon. The girls had no heart
to arrange No. 1 or do anything toward making it
comfortable, but lay on the bed in the midst of their
belongings, crying and receiving visits of condolence
from their friends. The S.S.U.C. meeting was put off.
Katy was in no humour to act as president, or Clover to
read her funny poem. Rose and Mary Silver sat by,
kissing them at intervals, and declaring that it was a
shame, while the other members dropped in one by one
to re-echo the same sentiments.

'If it had been anybody else!' said Alice Gibbons; 'but
Katy – Katy of all persons! It is too much!'

'So I told Mrs Florence,' sobbed Rose Red. 'Oh, why
was I born so bad? If I'd always been good, and a model
to the rest of you, perhaps she'd have believed me,
instead of scolding harder than ever.'

The idea of Rose as a 'model' made Clover smile in
the midst of her dolefulness.

'It's an outrageous thing,' said Ellen Gray, 'if Mrs
Florence only knew it, you two have done more to keep
the rest of us steady than any girls in school.'

'So they have,' blubbered Rose, whose pretty face was
quite swollen with crying. 'I've been getting better and
better every day since they came.' She put her arms
round Clover as she spoke, and sobbed harder than
ever.

It was in the midst of this excitement that Miss Jane saw fit to come in and 'inspect the room'. When she saw the crying girls and the general confusion of everything, she was very angry.

'I shall mark you both for disorder,' she said. 'Get off the bed, Miss Carr. Hang your dresses up at once, Clover, and put your shoes away. I never saw anything so disgraceful. All these things must be in order when I return, fifteen minutes from now, or I shall report you to Mrs Florence.'

'It's of no consequence what you do. We are not going to stay,' muttered Katy. But soon she was ashamed of having said this. Her anger was melting, and grief taking its place. 'Oh, papa! papa! Elsie! Elsie!' she whispered to herself, as she slowly hung up the dresses; and, unseen by the girls, she hid her face in the folds of Clover's grey alpaca, and shed some hot tears. Till then she had been too angry to cry.

This softer mood followed her all through the evening. Clover and Rose sat by, talking over the affair, and keeping their wrath warm with discussion. Katy said hardly a word. She felt too weary and depressed to speak.

'Who could have written the note?' asked Clover again and again. It was impossible to guess. It seemed absurd to suspect any of the older girls; but then, as Rose suggested, the absurdity as well as the signature might have been imitated to avoid detection.

'I know one thing,' remarked Rose, 'and that is that I should like to kill Mrs Searles. Horrid old thing! – peeping and prying into pockets. She has no business to be alive at all.'

Rose's ferocious speeches always sounded specially comical when taken in connection with her pink cheeks and her dimples.

'Shall you write to papa tonight, Katy?' asked Clover.

Katy shook her head. She was too heavy-hearted to talk. Big tears rolled down unseen and fell upon the pillow. After Rose was gone, and the candle out, she cried herself to sleep.

Waking early in the dim dawn, she lay and thought it over, Clover slumbering soundly beside her meanwhile. 'Morning brings counsel,' says the old proverb. In this case it seemed true. Katy, to her surprise, found a train of fresh thoughts filling her mind, which were not there when she fell asleep. She recalled her passionate words and feelings of the day before. Now that the mood had passed, they seemed to her worse than the injury which provoked them. Quick-tempered and generous people often experience this. It was easier for Katy to forgive Mrs Florence, because it was needful also that she should forgive herself.

'I said I would write to papa to take us away,' she thought. 'Why did I say that? What good would it do? It wouldn't make anybody disbelieve this horrid story. They'd only think I wanted to get away because I was found out. And papa would be so worried and disappointed. It has cost him a great deal to get us ready and send us here, and he wants us to stay a year. If we went home now, all the money would be wasted. And yet how horrid it is going to be after this! I don't feel as if I could ever bear to see Mrs Florence again. I must write.'

'But then,' her thoughts flowed on, 'home wouldn't

seem like home if we went away from school in disgrace, and knew that everybody here was believing such things. Suppose, instead, I were to write to papa to come on and make things straight. He'd find out the truth, and force Mrs Florence to see it. It would be very expensive, though; and I know he oughtn't to leave home again so soon. Oh, dear! How hard it is to know what to do!'

'What would Cousin Helen say?' she continued, going in imagination to the sofa-side of the dear friend who was to her like a second conscience. She shut her eyes and invented a long talk – her questions, Cousin Helen's replies. But, as everybody knows, it is impossible to play croquet by yourself and be strictly impartial to all the four balls. Katy found that she was making Cousin Helen play (that is, answer) as she herself wished, and not, as something whispered, she would answer were she really there.

'It is just the "Little Scholar" over again,' she said, half aloud, 'I can't see. I don't know how to act.' She remembered the dream she once had, of a great beautiful face and a helping hand. 'And it was real,' she murmured, 'and just as real, and just as near, now as then.'

The result of this long meditation was that, when Clover woke up, she found Katy leaning over, ready to kiss her for good morning, and looking bright and determined.

'Clovy,' she said, 'I've been thinking; and I'm not going to write to papa about this affair at all!'

'Are you not? Why not?' asked Clover, puzzled.

'Because it would worry him, and be of no use. He would come and take us right away, I'm sure; but Mrs Florence and all the teachers, and a great many of the girls, would always believe that this horrid, ridiculous story is true. I can't bear to have them. Let's stay, instead, and convince them that it isn't. I think we can.'

'I would a great deal rather go home,' said Clover. 'It won't ever be nice here again. We shall have this nasty room, and Miss Jane will be more horrid than ever, and the girls will think you wrote that note, and Lilly Page will say hateful things!' She buttoned her boots with a vindictive air.

'Never mind,' said Katy, trying to feel brave. 'I don't suppose it will be pleasant, but I'm pretty sure it's right. And Rosy and all the girls we really care for know how it is.'

'I can't bear it,' sighed Clover, with tears in her eyes. 'It is so cruel that they should say things about you.'

'I mean that they shall say something quite different before we go away,' replied Katy, stroking her hair. 'Cousin Helen would tell us to stay, I'm pretty sure. I was thinking about her just now, and I seemed to hear her voice in the air, saying over and over, "Live it down! Live it down! Live it down!" ' She half sang this, and took two or three dancing steps across the room.

'What a girl you are!' said Clover, consoled by seeing Katy look so bright.

Mrs Florence was surprised that morning, as she sat in her room, by the appearance of Katy. She looked pale, but perfectly quiet and gentle.

'Mrs Florence,' she said, 'I've come to say that I shall not write to my father to take us away, as I told you I should.'

Mrs Florence bowed stiffly, by way of answer.

'Not,' went on Katy, with a little flash in her eyes,

'that he would hesitate, or doubt my word one moment, if I did. But he wished us to stay here a year, and I don't wish to disappoint him. I'd rather stay. And, Mrs Florence, I'm sorry I spoke as I did yesterday. It was not right; but I was angry, and felt that you were unjust.'

'And today you own that I was not?'

'Oh, no!' replied Katy, 'I can't do that. You were unjust, because neither Clover nor I wrote that note. We would not do such a horrid thing for the world, and I hope some day you will believe us. But I ought not to have spoken so.'

Katy's face and voice were so truthful as she said this, that Mrs Florence was almost shaken in her opinion.

'We will say no more about the matter,' she remarked in a kinder tone. 'If your conduct is perfectly correct in future, it will go far to make this forgotten.'

Few things are more aggravating than to be forgiven when one has done no wrong. Katy felt this as she walked away from Mrs Florence's room. But she would not let herself grow angry again. 'Live it down!' she whispered, as she went into the school-room.

She and Clover had a good deal to endure for the next two or three weeks. They missed their old room with its sunny window and pleasant outlook. They missed Rose, who, down at the far end of Quaker Row, could not drop in half so often as had been her custom. Miss Jane was specially grim and sharp; and some of the upstairs girls, who resented Katy's plain speaking, and the formation of a society against flirting, improved the chance to be provoking. Lilly Page was one of these. She didn't really believe Katy guilty, but she liked to tease her by pretending to believe it.

'Only to think of the President of the Saintly Stuck-up Society being caught like this!' she remarked, maliciously. 'What are our great reformers coming to? Now if it had been a sinner like me, no one would be surprised!'

All this naturally was vexatious. Even sunny Clover shed many tears in private over her mortifications. But the girls bore their trouble bravely, and never said one syllable about the matter in the letters home. There were consolations, too, mixed with the annoyances. Rose Red clung to her two friends closely, and loyally fought their battles. The S.S.U.C. to a girl rallied round its chief. After that sad Saturday the meetings were resumed with as much spirit as ever. Katy's steadiness and uniform politeness and sweet temper impressed even those who would have been glad to believe a tale against her, and in a short time the affair ceased to be a subject for discussion, – was almost forgotten, in fact, except for a sore spot in Katy's heart, and one page in Rose Red's album, upon which, under the date of that fatal day, were written these words, headed by an appalling skull and cross-bones in pen-and-ink:

'N. B. – Pay Miss Jane off.'

CHANGES

'Clover, where's Clover?' cried Rose Red, popping her head into the schoolroom, where Katy sat writing her composition. 'Oh, Katy! there you are. I want you too. Come down to my room right away. I've such a thing to tell you.'

'What is it? Tell me too!' said Bella Arkwright. Bella was a veritable 'little pitcher', of the kind mentioned in the Proverb, and had an insatiable curiosity to know everything that other people knew.

'Tell you, miss? I should really like to know why!' replied Rose, who was not at all fond of Bella.

'You're real mean, and real unkind,' whined Bella. 'You think you're a great grown-up lady, and can have secrets. But you ain't! You're a little girl too – most as little as me. So there!'

Rose made a face at her, and a sort of growling rush, which had the effect of sending Bella screaming down the hall. Then, returning to the schoolroom –

'Do come, Katy,' she said; 'find Clover, and hurry! Really and truly I want you. I feel as if I should burst if

I don't tell somebody right away what I've found out.'

Katy began to be curious. She went in pursuit of Clover, who was practising in one of the recitation-rooms, and the three girls ran together down Quaker Row.

'Now,' said Rose, locking the door, and pushing forward a chair for Katy and another for Clover, 'swear that you won't tell, for this is a real secret – the greatest secret that ever was, and Mrs Florence would flay me alive if she knew that I knew!' She paused to enjoy the effect of her words, and suddenly began to snuff the air in a peculiar manner.

'Girls,' she said, solemnly, 'that little wretch of a Bella is in this room. I am sure of it.'

'What makes you think so?' cried the others, surprised.

'I smell that dreadful pomatum that she puts on her hair! Don't you notice it? She's hidden somewhere.' Rose looked sharply about for a minute, then made a pounce, and from under the bed dragged a small kicking heap. It was the guilty Bella.

'What were you doing there, you bad child?' demanded Rose, seizing the kicking feet and holding them fast.

'I don't care,' blubbered Bella, 'you wouldn't tell me your secret. You're a real horrid girl, Rose Red. I don't love you a bit.'

'Your affection is not a thing which I particularly pine for,' retorted Rose, seating herself, and holding the culprit before her by the ends of her short pig-tails. 'I don't want little girls who peep and hide to love me. I'd rather they wouldn't. Now listen. Do you know what I shall do if you ever come again into my room without leave? First, I shall cut off your hair, pomatum and all, with my pen-knife' – Bella screamed – 'and then I'll turn myself into a bear – a great brown bear – and eat you up!' Rose pronounced this threat with tremendous energy, and accompanied it with a snarl which showed all her teeth. Bella roared with fright, twitched away her pig-tails, unlocked the door and fled, Rose not pursuing her, but sitting comfortably in her chair and growling at intervals, till her victim was out of hearing. Then she rose and bolted the door again.

'How lucky that the imp is so fond of that smelly pomatum!' she remarked; 'one always knows where to look for her. It's as good as a bell round her neck! Now for the secret. You promise not to tell? Well, then, Mrs Florence is going away week after next, and, what's more – she's going to be married!'

'Not really!' cried the others.

'Really and truly. She's going to be married to a clergy-man.'

'How did you find out?'

'Why, it's the most curious thing. You know my blue lawn, which Miss James is making? This morning I went to try it on, Miss Barnes with me of course, and while Miss James was fitting the waist Mrs Seccomb came in and sat down on the sofa by Miss Barnes. They began to talk, and pretty soon Mrs Seccomb said, 'What day does Mrs Florence go?'

' "Thursday week," said Miss Barnes. She sort of mumbled it, and looked to see if I were listening. I wasn't; but of course after that I did – as hard as I could.

' "And where does the important event take place?"

asked Mrs Seccomb. She's so funny with her little bit of a mouth and her long words. She always looks as if each of them was a big pill, and she wanted to swallow it and couldn't.'

' "In Lewisberg, at her sister's house," said Miss Barnes. She mumbled more than ever, but I heard.

' "What a deplorable loss she will be to our limited circle!" said Mrs Seccomb. I couldn't imagine what they meant. But don't you think, when I got home there was this letter from Sylvia, and she says, "Your adored Mrs Florence is going to be married. I'm afraid you'll all break your hearts about it. Mother met the gentleman at a party the other night. She says he looks clever, but isn't at all handsome, which is a pity, for Mrs Florence is a raving beauty in my opinion. He's an excellent preacher, we hear; and won't she manage the parish to perfection? How shall you like being left to the tender mercies of Mrs Nipson?" Now did you ever hear anything so droll in your life?' went on Rose, folding up her letter. 'Just think of those two things coming together the same day! It's like a sum in arithmetic, with an answer which "proves" the sum, isn't it?'

Rose had counted on producing an effect, and she certainly was not disappointed. The girls could think and talk of nothing else for the remainder of that afternoon.

It was a singular fact that before two days were over, every scholar in the school knew that Mrs Florence was going to be married! How the secret got out nobody could guess. Rose protested that it wasn't her fault – she had been a miracle of discretion, a perfect sphinx; but there was a guilty laugh in her eyes, and Katy suspected that the sphinx had unbent a little. Nothing so exciting had ever happened at the Nunnery before. Some of the older scholars were quite inconsolable. They bemoaned themselves, and got together in corners to enjoy the luxury of woe. Nothing comforted them but the project of getting up a 'testimonial' for Mrs Florence.

What this testimonial should be caused great discussion in the school. Everybody had a different idea, and everybody was sure that her idea was better than anybody else's. All the school contributed. The money collected amounted to nearly forty dollars, and the question was, what should be bought?

Every sort of thing was proposed. Lilly Page insisted that nothing could possibly be so appropriate as a bouquet of wax flowers and a glass shade to put over it. There was a strong party in favour of spoons. Annie Silsbie suggested 'a statue'; somebody else a clock. Rose Red was for a cabinet piano, and Katy had some trouble in convincing her that forty dollars would not buy one. Bella demanded that they should get 'an organ'.

'You can go along with it as monkey,' said Rose, which remark made Bella caper with indignation.

At last, after long discussion and some quarrelling, a cake-basket was fixed upon. Sylvia Redding happened to be making a visit in Boston, and Rose was commissioned to write and ask her to select the gift and send it up by express. The girls could hardly wait.

'I do hope it will be pretty, don't you?' they said over and over again.

When the box arrived, they all gathered to see it opened. Esther Dearborn took out the nails, half-a-dozen hands lifted the lid, and Rose unwrapped the tissue-paper and displayed the basket up to general view.

'Oh, what a beauty!' cried everybody.

It was woven of twisted silver wire. Two figures of children with wings and garlands supported the handle on either side. In the middle of the handle were a pair of silver doves, billing and cooing in the most affectionate way, over a tiny shield, on which were engraved Mrs Florence's initials.

'I never saw one like it!' 'Doesn't it look heavy?' 'Rose Red, your sister is splendid!' cried a chorus of voices, as Rose, highly gratified, held up the basket.

'Who shall present it?' asked Louisa Agnew. 'Rose Red,' said some of the girls.

'No, indeed, I'm not tall enough,' protested Rose, 'it must be somebody who'd kind of sweep into the room and be impressive. I vote for Katy.'

'Oh, no!' said Katy, shrinking back, 'I shouldn't do it well at all. Suppose we put it to vote?'

Ellen Gray cut some slips of paper, and each girl wrote a name and dropped it into a box. When the votes were counted, Katy's name appeared on all but three.

'I propose that we make this vote unanimous,' said Rose, highly delighted.

The girls agreed; and Rose, jumping on a chair, exclaimed –

'Three cheers for Katy Carr! Keep time, girls, – one, two, hip, hip, hurrah!'

The hurrahs were given with enthusiasm, for Katy, almost without knowing it, had become popular. She was too much touched to speak at first. When she did, it was to protest against her election.

'Esther would do it beautifully,' she said, 'and I think Mrs Florence would like the basket better if she gave it. You know ever since –' she stopped. Even now she could not refer with composure to the affair of the note.

'Oh,' cried Louisa, 'she's thinking of that ridiculous note Mrs Florence made such a fuss about. As if anybody supposed you wrote it, Katy! I don't believe even Miss Jane is such a goose as that. Anyway, if she is, that's one reason more why you should present the basket, to show that we don't think so.' She gave Katy a kiss by way of period.

'Yes, indeed, you're chosen, and you must give it,' cried the others.

'Very well,' said Katy, extremely gratified, 'what am I to say?'

'We'll compose a speech for you,' replied Rose. 'Sugar your voice, Katy, and, whatever you do, stand up straight. Don't crook over, as if you thought you were tall. It's a bad trick you have, child, and I'm always sorry to see it,' concluded Rose, with the air of a wise mamma giving a lecture.

It is droll how much can go on in a school unseen and unsuspected by its teachers. Mrs Florence never dreamed that the girls had guessed her secret. Her plan was to go away as if for a visit, and leave Mrs Nipson to explain at her leisure. She was therefore quite un- prepared for the appearance of Katy holding the beauti- ful basket, which was full of fresh roses, crimson, white, and pink. I am afraid the rules of the S.S.U.C. had been slightly relaxed to allow of Rose Red's getting these flowers; certainly they grew nowhere in Hillsover except in Professor Seccomb's garden.

'The girls wanted me to give you this, with a great

deal of love from us all,' said Katy, feeling strangely embarrassed, and hardly venturing to raise her eyes. She set the basket on the table. 'We hope so much that you will be happy,' she added in a low voice, and moved towards the door.

Mrs Florence had been too much surprised to speak, but now she called, 'Wait! Come back a moment.'

Katy came back. Mrs Florence's cheeks were flushed. She looked very handsome. Katy almost thought there were tears in her eyes.

'Tell the girls that I thank them very much. Their present is beautiful. I shall always value it!'

She blushed as she spoke, and Katy blushed too. It made her shy to see the usually composed Mrs Florence so confused.

'What did she say? what did she say?' demanded the others, who were collected in groups round the school-room door to hear a report of the interview.

Katy repeated the message. Some of the girls were disappointed.

'Is that all?' they said. 'We thought she would stand up and make a speech.'

'Or a short poem,' put in Rose Red – 'a few stanzas thrown off on the spur of the moment; like this, for instance –

> "Thank you, kindly, for your basket,
> Which I didn't mean to ask it;
> But I'll very gladly take it,
> And when 'tis full of cake, it
> Will frequently remind me
> Of the girls I left behind me!"'

There was a universal giggle, which brought Miss Jane out of the school-room.

'Order!' she said, ringing the bell. 'Young ladies, what are you about? Study hour has begun.'

'We're so sorry Mrs Florence is going away,' said some of the girls.

'How did you know that she is going?' demanded Miss Jane sharply.

Nobody answered.

Next day Mrs Florence left. Katy saw her go with a secret regret.

'If only she would have said that she didn't believe I wrote that note!' she told Clover.

'I don't care what she believes! She's a stupid, unjust woman!' replied independent little Clover.

Mrs Nipson was now in sole charge of the establishment. She had never tried schoolkeeping before, and had various pet plans and theories of her own, which she had only been waiting Mrs Florence's departure to put into practice.

One of these was that the school was to dine three times a week on pudding and bread and butter. Mrs Nipson had a theory – very convenient and economical for herself, but highly distasteful to her scholars – that it was injurious for young people to eat meat every day in hot weather.

The puddings were made of batter, with a sprinkling of blackberries or raisins. Now, rising at six, and studying four hours and a half on a light breakfast, has a wonderful effect on the appetite, as all who have tried it will testify. The poor girls would go down to dinner as hungry as wolves, and eye the large, pale slices on their plates with a wrath and dismay which I cannot pretend to describe. Very thick the slices were, and there was plenty of thin, sugared sauce to eat with them, and plenty of bread and butter; but somehow, the whole was unsatisfying, and the hungry girls would go upstairs almost as ravenous as when they came down. The second-table-ites were always hanging over the balusters to receive them, and when to the demand, 'What did you have for dinner?' 'Pudding!' was answered, a low groan would run from one to another, and a general gloom seemed to drop down and envelop the party.

It may have been in consequence of this experience of starvation that the orders for Fourth of July were that year so unusually large. It was an old custom in the school that the girls should celebrate the National Independence by buying as many goodies as they liked. There was no candy shop in Hillsover, so Mrs Nipson took the orders, and sent to Boston for the things, which were charged on the bills with other extras. Under these blissful circumstances, the girls felt that they could afford to be extravagant, and made out their list regardless of expense. Rose Red's, for this Fourth, ran thus:

> Two pounds of Chocolate Caramels.
> Two pounds of Sugar Almonds.
> Two pounds of Lemon Drops.
> Two pounds of Mixed Candy.
> Two pounds of Macaroons.
> A dozen Oranges.
> A dozen Lemons.
> A drum of Figs.
> A box of French Plums.
> A loaf of Almond Cake.

The result of this liberal order was that, after the great wash-baskets of parcels had been distributed, and the school had rioted for twenty-four hours upon these unaccustomed luxuries, Rose was found lying on her bed, ghastly and pallid.

'Never speak to me of anything sweet again so long as I live!' she gasped. 'Talk of vinegar, or pickles, or sour apples; but don't allude to sugar in any form, if you love me! Oh, why, why did I send for those fatal things?'

In time all the candy was eaten up, and the school went back to its normal condition. Three weeks later came College Commencement.

'Are you and Clover Craters or Symposiums?' demanded Lilly Page, meeting Katy in the hall, a few days before this important event.

'What do you mean?'

'Why, has nobody told you about them? They are the two great College Societies. All the girls belong to one or the other, and make the wreaths to dress their halls. We work up in the Gymnasium; the Crater girls take the east side, and the Symposium girls the west, and when the wreaths grow too long we hang them out of the windows. It's the greatest fun in the world! Be a Symposium, do! I'm one!'

'I shall have to think about it before deciding,' said Katy, privately resolving to join Rose Red's Society, whichever it was. The Crater it proved to be, so Katy and Clover enrolled themselves with the Craters. Three days before Commencement wreath-making began. The afternoons were wholly given up to the work, and, instead of walking, or piano practice, the girls sat plaiting oak-leaves into garlands many yards long. Baskets of fresh leaves were constantly brought in, and there was a strife between the rival Societies as to which should accomplish most.

It was great fun, as Lilly had said, to sit there amid the green boughs, and pleasant leafy smells, a buzz of gay voices in the air, and a general sense of holiday. The Gymnasium would have furnished many a pretty picture for an artist during those three afternoons, only, unfortunately, no artist was let in to see it.

One day, Rose Red, emptying a basket, lighted upon a white parcel, hidden beneath the leaves.

'Lemon drops!' she exclaimed, applying a finger and thumb with all the dexterity of Jack Horner. 'Here, Crater girls, here's something for you! Don't you pity the Symposiums?'

But next day a big package of peppermints appeared in the Symposium basket, so neither Society could boast advantage over the other. They were pretty nearly equal, too, in the quantity of wreath made – the Craters' measuring nine hundred yards, and the Symposiums' nine hundred and two. As for the Halls, which they were taken over to see the evening before Commencement, it was impossible to say which was most beautifully trimmed. Each faction preferred its own, and President Searles said that both did the young ladies credit.

They all sat in the gallery of the church on Commencement Day, and heard the speeches. It was very hot, and the speeches were not exactly interesting, being on such subjects as 'The Influence of a Republic on Men of Letters,' and 'The Abstract Law of Justice, as applied to Human Affairs'; but the music, and the crowd, and the spectacle of six hundred ladies all fanning themselves at once, were entertaining, and the girls would not have missed them for the world. Later in the day another diversion was afforded them by the throngs of pink and blue ladies and white-gloved gentlemen who passed the house on their way to the President's Levée; but they were not allowed to enjoy this amusement long, for Miss Jane, suspecting what was going on, went from room to room, and ordered everybody summarily off to bed.

With the close of Commencement Day, a deep sleep seemed to settle over Hillsover. Most of the Professors' families went off to enjoy themselves at the mountains or at the sea-side, leaving their houses shut up. This gave the village a drowsy and deserted air. There were no boys playing ball on the Common, or swinging on the College fence; no look of life in the streets. The weather continued warm, the routine of study and exercise grew dull, and teachers and scholars alike were glad when the middle of September arrived, and with it the opening of the autumn vacation.

THE AUTUMN VACATION

The last day of term was one of confusion. Every part of the house was given over to trunks and packing. Mrs Nipson sat at her desk, making out bills, and listening to requests about rooms and room-mates. Miss Jane counted books and atlases, taking note of each ink-spot and dog-eared page. The girls ran about, searching for missing articles, deciding what to take home and what to leave, engaging each other for the winter walks. All rules were laid aside. The sober Nunnery seemed turned into a hive of buzzing bees. Bella slid twice down the baluster of the front stairs without being reproved; and Rose Red threw her arm round Katy's waist, and waltzed the whole length of Quaker Row.

'I'm so happy, that I should like to scream!' she announced, as their last whirl brought them up against the wall. 'Isn't vacation just lovely? Katy, you don't look half glad.'

'We're not going home, you know,' replied Katy, in a rather doleful tone. She and Clover were not so enraptured at the coming of vacation as the rest of the girls.

Spending a month with Mrs Page and Lilly was by no means the same thing as spending it with papa and the children.

Next morning, however, when the big stage drove up, and the girls crowded in; when Mrs Nipson stood in the doorway, blandly waving farewell, and the maids flourished their dusters out of the upper windows, they found themselves sharing the general excitement, and joining heartily in the cheer which arose as the stage moved away. The girls felt so happy and good-natured, that some of them even kissed their hands to Miss Jane.

Such a wild company is not often met with on a railroad train. They all went together as far as the Junction; and Mr Gray, Ellen's father, who had been put in charge of the party by Mrs Nipson, had his hands full to keep them in any sort of order. He was a timid old gentleman, and, as Rose suggested, his expression resembled that of a sedate hen who suddenly finds herself responsible for the conduct of a brood of ducklings.

'My dear, my dear!' he feebly remonstrated, 'would you buy any more candy? Do you not think so many pea-nuts may be bad for you?'

'Oh, no, sir!' replied Rose; 'they never hurt me a bit; I can eat thousands!' Then, as a stout lady entered the car, and made a motion toward the vacant seat beside her, she rolled her eyes wildly, and said, 'Excuse me, but perhaps I had better take the end seat, so as to get out easily in case I have a fit.'

'Fits!' cried the stout lady, and walked away with the utmost despatch. Rose gave a wicked chuckle, the girls tittered, and Mr Gray visibly trembled.

'Is she really afflicted in this way?' he whispered.

'Oh, no, papa! it's only Rose's nonsense!' apologized Ellen, who was laughing as hard as the rest. But Mr Gray did not feel comfortable, and he was very glad when they reached the Junction, and half of his troublesome charge departed on the branch road.

At six o'clock they arrived in Springfield. Half-a-dozen papas were waiting for their daughters; trains stood ready; there was a clamour of good-byes. Mr Page was absorbed by Lilly, who kissed him incessantly, and chattered so fast that he had no eyes for anyone else. Louisa was borne away by an uncle, with whom she was to pass the night; and Katy and Clover found themselves left alone. They did not like to interrupt Lilly, so they retreated to a bench, and sat down feeling rather left out and homesick; and, though they did not say so, I am sure that each was thinking about papa.

It was only for a moment. Mr Page spied them, and came forward with such a kind greeting, that the forlorn feeling fled at once. They were to pass the night at the Massasoit, it seemed; and he collected their bags, and led the way across the street to the hotel, where rooms were already engaged for them.

'Now for waffles,' whispered Lilly, as they went upstairs; and when, after a few minutes of washing and brushing, they came down again into the dining-room, she called for so many things, and announced herself 'starved' in such a tragical tone, that two amused waiters at once flew to the rescue, and devoted themselves to supplying her wants. Waffle after waffle – each hotter and crisper than the last – did those long-suffering men produce, till even Lilly's appetite gave out, and she was forced to own that she could not swallow another morsel. This climax reached, they went into the parlour; and the girls sat down in the window to watch the people in the street – which, after quiet Hillsover, looked as brilliant and crowded as Broadway.

There were not many persons in the parlour. A grave-looking couple sat at a table at some distance, and a pretty little boy in a velvet jacket was playing around the room. He seemed about five years old; and Katy, who was fond of children, put out her hand as he went by, caught him, and lifted him into her lap. He did not seem shy, but looked her in the face composedly, like a grown person.

'What is your name, dear?' she asked.

'Daniel D'Aubigny Sparks,' answered the little boy. His voice was prim and distinct.

'Do you live at this hotel?'

'Yes, ma'am. I reside here with my father and mother.'

'And what do you do all day? Are there some other little boys for you to play with?'

'I do not wish to play with any little boys,' replied Daniel D'Aubigny, in a dignified tone. 'I prefer to be with my parents. Today we have taken a walk. We went to see a beautiful conservatory outside the city. There is a Victoria Regia there. I had often heard of this wonderful lily; and in the last number of the London "Musée" there is a picture of it, represented with a small negro child standing upon one of its leaves. My father said that he did not think this possible; but when we saw the plant, we perceived that the print was not an exaggeration. Such is the size of the leaf, that a small negro child might very easily be supported upon it.'

'Oh, my!' cried Katy, feeling as if she had accidentally picked up an elderly gentleman, or a college professor. 'Pray, how old are you?'

'Nearly nine, ma'am,' replied the little fellow, with a bow.

Katy, too much appalled for farther speech, let him slide off her lap. But Mr Page, who was much diverted, continued the conversation; and Daniel, mounting a chair, crossed his short legs, and discoursed with all the gravity of an old man. The talk was principally about himself – his tastes, his adventures, his ideas about art and science. Now and then he alluded to his papa and mamma, and once to his grandfather.

'My maternal grandfather,' he said, 'was a remarkable man. In his youth he spent a great deal of time in France. He was there at the time of the French Revolution, and, as it happened, was present at the execution of the unfortunate Queen Marie Antoinette. This, of course, was not intentional. It chanced thus. My grandfather was in a barber's shop, having his hair cut. He saw a great crowd going by, and went out to ask what was the cause. The crowd was so immense that he could not extricate himself; he was carried along against his will, and not only so, but was forced to the front and compelled to witness every part of the dreadful scene. He has often told my mother that, after the execution, the executioner held up the queen's head to the people: the eyes were open, and there was in them an expression, not of pain, not of fear, but of great astonishment and surprise.'

This anecdote carried 'great astonishment and surprise' into the company who listened to it. Mr Page gave a sort of chuckle, and saying, 'By George!' got up and left the room. The girls put their heads out of the window that they might laugh unseen. Daniel gazed at their shaking shoulders with an air of wonder, while the grave couple at the end of the room, who for some moments had been looking disturbed, drew near and informed the youthful prodigy that it was time for him to go to bed.

'Good-night, young ladies,' said the small condescending voice. Katy alone had 'presence of countenance' enough to return this salutation. It was a relief to find that Daniel went to bed at all.

Next morning at breakfast they saw him seated between his parents, eating bread and milk. He bowed to them over the edge of the bowl.

'Dreadful little prig! They should bottle him in spirits of wine as a specimen. It's the only thing he'll ever be fit for,' remarked Mr Page, who rarely said so sharp a thing about anybody.

Louisa joined them at the station. She was to travel under Mr Page's care, and Katy was much annoyed at Lilly's manner to her. It grew colder and less polite with every mile. By the time they reached Ashburn it was absolutely rude.

'Come and see me very soon, girls,' said Louisa, as they parted in the station. 'I long to have you know mother and little Daisy. Oh, there's papa!' and she rushed up to a tall, pleasant-looking man, who kissed her fondly, shook hands with Mr Page, and touched his hat to Lilly, who scarcely bowed in return.

'Boarding-school is so horrid,' she remarked, 'you get

all mixed up with people you don't want to know – people not in society at all.'

'How can you talk such nonsense?' said her father; 'the Agnews are thoroughly respectable, and Mr Agnew is one of the cleverest men I know.'

Katy was pleased when Mr Page said this, but Lilly shrugged her shoulders and looked cross.

'Papa is so democratic,' she whispered to Clover, 'he don't care a bit who people are, so long as they are respectable and clever.'

'Well, why should he?' replied Clover. Lilly was more disgusted than ever.

Ashburn was a large and prosperous town. It was built on the slopes of a picturesque hill, and shaded with fine elms. As they drove through the streets, Katy and Clover caught glimpses of conservatories and shrubberies, and beautiful houses with bay windows and piazzas.

'That's ours,' said Lilly, as the carriage turned in at the gate. It stopped, and Mr Page jumped out.

'Here we are,' he said. 'Gently, Lilly, you'll hurt yourself. Well, my dears, we're very glad to see you in our home at last.'

This was kind and comfortable, and the girls were glad of it, for the size and splendour of the house quite dazzled and made them shy. They had never seen anything like it before. The hall had a marble floor, and busts, and statues. Large rooms opened on either side; and Mrs Page, who came forward to receive them, wore a heavy silk with a train and laces, and looked altogether as if she were dressed for a party.

'This is the drawing-room,' said Lilly, delighted to see the girls so impressed. 'Isn't it splendid?' And she led

the way into a stiff, chilly, magnificent apartment, where
all the blinds were closed, and all the shades pulled
down, and all the furniture shrouded in linen covers.
Even the picture-frames and mirrors were sewed up in
muslin to keep off flies; and the bronzes and alabaster
ornaments on the chimney-piece and *étagère* gleamed
through the dim light in a ghostly way. Katy thought it
very dismal. She couldn't imagine anybody sitting down
there to read or sew, or do anything pleasant, and
probably it was not intended that any one should do so;
for Mrs Page soon showed them out, and led the way
into a smaller room at the back of the hall.

'Well, Katy,' she said, 'how do you like Hillsover?'

'Very well, ma'am,' replied Katy; but she did not speak
enthusiastically.

'Ah!' said Mrs Page, shaking her head, 'it takes time
to shake off home habits, and to learn to get along with
young people after living with older ones and catching
their ways. You'll like it better as you go on.'

Katy privately doubted whether this was true, but she
did not say so. Pretty soon Lilly offered to show them
upstairs to their room. She took them first into three
large and elegant chambers, which she explained were
kept for grand company, and then into a much smaller
one in a wing.

'Mother always puts my friends in here,' she remarked; 'she says it's plenty good enough for school-
girls to thrash about in!'

'What does she mean?' cried Clover indignantly, as
Lilly closed the door. 'We don't thrash!'

'I can't imagine,' answered Katy, who was vexed too.
But pretty soon she began to laugh.

'People are so funny,' she said. 'Never mind, Clovy, this room is good enough, I'm sure.'

'Must we unpack, or will it do to go down in our alpacas?' asked Clover.

'I don't know,' replied Katy, in a doubtful tone. 'Perhaps we had better change our gowns. Cousin Olivia always dresses so much! Here's your blue muslin right on top of the trunk. You might put on that, and I'll wear my purple.'

The girls were glad they had done this, for it was evidently expected, and Lilly had dressed her hair and donned a fresh white piqué. Mrs Page examined their dresses, and said that Clover's was a lovely blue, but that ruffles were quite gone out, and everything must be made with basques. She supposed they needed quantities of things, and she had already engaged a dressmaker for them.

'Thank you,' said Katy, 'but I don't think we need anything. We had our winter dresses made before we left home.'

'Winter dresses! last spring! My dear, what were you thinking of? They must be completely out of fashion.'

'You can't think how little Hillsover people know about fashions,' replied Katy, laughing.

'But, my dear, for your own sake!' exclaimed Mrs Page, distressed by these lax remarks. 'I'll look over your things tomorrow and see what you need.'

Katy did not dare to say 'No,' but she felt rebellious. When they were half through tea, the door opened, and a boy came in.

'You are late, Clarence,' said Mr Page, while Mrs Page frowned, and observed, 'Clarence makes a point of being late. He really deserves to be made to go without his supper. Shut the door, Clarence. O mercy! don't bang it in that way. I wish you would learn to shut a door properly. Here are your cousins, Katy and Clover Carr. Now let me see if you can shake hands with them like a gentleman, and not like a ploughboy.'

Clarence, a square, freckled boy of thirteen, with reddish hair, and a sort of red sparkle in his eyes, looked very angry at this address. He did not offer to shake hands at all, but elevating his shoulders said, 'How d'you do!' in a sulky voice, and sitting down at the table buried his nose without delay in a glass of milk. His mother gave a disgusted sigh.

'What a boy you are!' she said. 'Your cousins will think that you have never been taught anything, which is not the case; for I'm sure I've taken twice the pains with you that I have with Lilly. Pray excuse him, Katy. It's no use trying to make boys polite!'

'Isn't it?' said Katy, thinking of Phil and Dorry, and wondering what Mrs Page could mean.

'Hullo, Lilly!' broke in Clarence, spying his sister as it seemed for the first time.

'How d'you do?' said Lilly, carelessly. 'I was wondering how long it would be before you would condescend to notice my existence.'

'I didn't see you.'

'I know you didn't. I never knew such a boy! You might as well have no eyes at all.'

Clarence scowled, and went on with his supper. His mother seemed unable to let him alone. 'Clarence, don't take such large mouthfuls! Clarence, pray use your napkin! Clarence, your elbows are on the table sir! Now,

Clarence, don't try to speak until you have swallowed all that bread' – came every other moment. Katy felt very sorry for Clarence. His manners were certainly bad, but it seemed quite dreadful that public attention should be thus constantly called to them.

The evening was rather dull. There was a sort of put-in-order-for-company air about the parlour, which made everybody stiff. Mrs Page did not sew or read, but sat in a low chair looking like a lady in a fashion-plate, and asked questions about Hillsover, some of which were not easy to answer, as, for example, 'Have you any other intimate friends among the school-girls beside Lilly?' About eight o'clock a couple of young, very young, gentlemen came in, at the sight of whom Lilly, who was half asleep, brightened and became lively and talkative. One of them was the Mr Hickman, whose father married Mr Page's sister-in-law's sister, thus making him in some mysterious way a 'first cousin' of Lilly's. He was an Arrowmouth student, and seemed to have so many jokes to laugh over with Lilly that before long they withdrew to a distant sofa, where they conversed in whispers. The other youth, introduced as Mr Eels, was left to entertain the other three ladies, which duty he performed by sucking the head of his cane in silence while they talked to him. He too was an Arrowmouth Sophomore.

In the midst of the conversation, the door, which stood ajar, opened a little wider, and a dog's head appeared, followed by a tail, which waggled so beseechingly for leave to come farther that Clover, who liked dogs, put out her hand and said, 'Come here, poor fellow!' The dog ran up to her at once. He was not pretty, being of a pepper-and-salt colour, with a blunt nose and no particular sort of a tail, but he looked good-natured; and Clover fondled him cordially, while Mr Eels took his cane out of his mouth to ask, 'What kind of a dog is that, Mrs Page?'

'I'm sure I don't know,' she replied; while Lilly, from the distance, added affectedly, 'Oh, he's the most dreadful dog, Mr Eels! My brother picked him up in the street, and none of us know the least thing about him, except that he's the commonest kind of a dog – a sort of cur, I believe.'

'That's not true!' broke in a stern voice from the hall, which made everybody jump; and Katy, looking that way, was aware of a vengeful eye glaring at Lilly through the crack of the door. 'He's a very valuable dog, indeed – half mastiff and half terrier, with a touch of bull-dog – so there, miss!'

The effect of this remark was startling. Lilly gave a scream; Mrs Page rose, and hurried to the door; while the dog, hearing his master's voice, rushed that way also, got before her, and almost threw her down. Katy and Clover could not help laughing, and Mr Eels meeting their amused eyes, removed the cane from his mouth, and grew conversible.

'That Clarence is a droll little chap!' he remarked, confidentially. 'Bright, too! He'd be a nice fellow if he wasn't picked at so much. It never does a fellow any good to be picked at – now does it, Miss Carr?'

'No; I don't think it does.'

'I say,' continued Mr Eels, 'I've seen you young ladies up at Hillsover, haven't I? Aren't you both at the Nunnery?'

'Yes. It's vacation now, you know.'

'I was sure I'd seen you. You had a room on the side next the President's, didn't you? I thought so. We fellows didn't know your names, so we called you the "The Real Nuns".'

'Real Nuns?'

'Yes, because you never looked out of the window at us. Real nuns and sham nuns – don't you see? Almost all the young ladies are sham nuns, except you, and two pretty little ones in the storey above, fifth window from the end.'

'Oh, I know!' said Clover, much amused. 'Sally Alsop, you know, Katy, and Amy Erskine. They are such nice girls.'

'Are they?' replied Mr Eels, with the air of one who notes down names for future reference. 'Well, I thought so. Not so much fun in them as some of the others, I guess; but a fellow likes other things as well as fun. I know if my sister was there I'd rather have her take the dull line than the other.'

Katy treasured up this remark for the benefit of the S.S.U.C. Mrs Page came back just then, and Mr Eels resumed his cane. Nothing more was heard of Clarence that night.

Next morning Cousin Olivia fulfilled her threat of inspecting the girls' wardrobe. She shook her head over the simple, untrimmed merinos and thick cloth coats.

'There's no help for it,' she said; 'but it's a great pity. You would much better have waited and had things fresh. Perhaps it may be possible to match the merino, and have some sort of basque arrangement added on. I will talk to Madame Chonfleur about it. Meantime I shall get one handsome thick dress for each of you, and have it stylishly made. That, at least, you really need.'

Katy was too glad to be so easily let off to raise objections. So that afternoon she and Clover were taken out to 'choose their material,' Mrs Page said, but really to sit by while she chose it for them. At the dressmaker's it was the same; they stood passive while the orders were given, and everything decided upon.

'Isn't it funny?' whispered Clover; 'but I don't like it a bit, do you? It's just like Elsie saying how she'll have her doll's things made.'

'Oh, this dress isn't mine! it's Cousin Olivia's!' replied Katy. 'She's welcome to have it trimmed just as she likes.'

But when the suits came home she was forced to be pleased. There was no over-trimming, no look of finery; everything fitted perfectly, and had the air of finish which they had noticed and admired in Lilly's clothes. Katy almost forgot that she had objected to the dresses as unnecessary.

'After all, it is nice to look nice,' she confessed to Clover.

Excepting to go to the dressmaker's, there was not much to amuse during the first half of vacation.

Mrs Page took them to drive now and then, and Katy found some pleasant books in the library, and read a good deal. Clover meantime made friends with Clarence. I think his heart was won that first evening by her attentions to Guest, the dog, that mysterious animal, 'half mastiff and half terrier, with a touch of the bull-dog.' Clarence loved Guest dearly, and was gratified that Clover liked him; for the poor animal had few friends in the household. In a little while Clarence became quite sociable with her, and tolerably so with Katy. They found him, as Mr Eels had said, 'a bright fellow,' and pleasant and good-humoured enough when taken in the right way. Lilly always seemed to take him wrong, and his treatment of her was most disagreeable, snappish, and quarrelsome to the last degree.

'Much you don't like oranges!' he said, one day at dinner, in answer to an innocent remark of hers. 'Much! I've seen you eat two at a time, without stopping. Pa, Lilly says she don't like oranges! I've seen her eat two at a time, without stopping! Much she doesn't! I've seen her eat two at a time, without stopping!' He kept this up for five minutes, looking from one person to another, and repeating, 'Much she don't! Much!' till Lilly was almost crying from vexation, and even Clover longed to box his ears. Nobody was sorry when Mr Page ordered him to leave the room, which he did with a last vindictive 'Much,' addressed to Lilly.

'How can Clarence behave so?' said Katy, when she and Clover were alone.

'I don't know,' replied Clover. 'He's such a nice boy sometimes; but when he isn't nice, he's the horridest boy I ever saw. I wish you'd talk to him, Katy, and tell him how dreadfully it sounds when he says such things.'

'No, indeed. He'd take it much better from you. You're nearer his age, and could do it nicely and pleasantly, and not make him feel as if he were being scolded. Poor fellow, he gets plenty of that!'

Clover said no more about the subject, but she meditated. She had a good deal of tact for so young a girl, and took care to get Clarence into a specially amicable mood before she began her lecture. 'Look here, you bad boy, how could you tease poor Lilly so yesterday? Guest, speak up, sir, and tell your massa how naughty it was!'

'Oh, dear! now you're going to nag!' growled Clarence, in an injured voice.

'No, I'm not – not the least in the world. I'll promise not to. But just tell me' – and Clover put her hand on the rough, red-brown hair, and stroked it – 'just tell me why you "go for to do" such things? They're not a bit nice.'

'Lilly's so hateful!' grumbled Clarence.

'Well, she is sometimes, I know,' admitted Clover, candidly. 'But because she is hateful is no reason why you should be unmanly.'

'Unmanly!' cried Clarence, flushing.

'Yes, I call it unmanly to tease and quarrel, and contradict like that. It's like girls. They do it sometimes, but I didn't think a boy would. I thought he'd be ashamed.'

'Doesn't Dorry ever quarrel or tease?' asked Clarence, who liked to hear about Clover's brothers and sisters.

'Not now, and never in that way. He used to sometimes, when he was little, but now he's real nice. He wouldn't speak to a girl as you speak to Lilly for anything. He'd think it wasn't being a gentleman.'

'Stuff about gentleman, and all that!' retorted Clarence. 'Mother dings the word into my ears till I hate it.'

'Well, it is rather teasing to be reminded all the time, I admit; but you can't wonder that your mother wants you to be a gentleman, Clarence. It's the best thing in the world, I think. I hope Phil and Dorry will grow up just like papa, for everybody says he's the most perfect gentleman, and it makes me so proud to hear them.'

'But what does it mean, anyway? Mother says it's how you hold your fork, and how you chew, and how you put on your hat. If that's all, I don't think it amounts to much.'

'Oh, that isn't all. It's being gentle, don't you see? Gentle and nice to everybody, and just as polite to poor people as to rich ones,' said Clover, talking fast, in her eagerness to explain her meaning – 'and never being selfish, or noisy, or pushing people out of their place. Forks, and hats, and all that are only little ways of making one's self more agreeable to other people. A gentleman is a gentleman inside, all through. Oh, I wish I could make you see what I mean!'

'Oh, that's it, is it?' said Clarence.

Whether he understood or not, Clover could not tell, or whether she had done any good or not; but she had the discretion to say no more; and certainly Clarence was not offended, for after that day he grew fonder of her than ever. Lilly became absolutely jealous. She had never cared particularly for Clarence's affection, but she did not like to have anyone preferred above herself.

'It's pretty hard, I think,' she told Clover. 'Clare does everything you tell him, and he treats me awfully. It isn't a bit fair! I'm his sister, and you're only a second cousin.'

All this time the girls had seen almost nothing of Louisa Agnew. She called once, but Lilly received the call with them, and was so cool and stiff that Louisa grew stiff also, and made but a short stay; and when the girls returned the visit she was out. A few days before the close of the vacation, however, a note came from her.

DEAR KATY,

I am so sorry not to have seen more of you and Clover. Won't you come and spend Wednesday with us? Mamma sends her love, and hopes you will come early, so as to have a long day, for she wants to know you. I long to show you the baby and everything. Do come. Papa will see you home in the evening. Remember me to Lilly. She has so many friends to see during vacation that I am sure she will forgive me for stealing you for one day.

Yours affectionately,

LOUISA

Katy thought this message very politely expressed; but Lilly, when she heard it, tossed her head, and said she 'really thought Miss Agnew might let her name alone when she wrote notes.' Mrs Page seemed to pity the girls for having to go. They must, she supposed, as it was a school-mate; but she feared it would be stupid for them. The Agnews were queer sort of people, not in society at all. Mr Agnew was clever, people said; but really, she knew very little about the family. Perhaps it would not do to decline.

Katy and Clover had no idea of declining. They sent a warm little note of acceptance, and on the appointed day set off bright and early with a good deal of pleasant anticipation. The vacation had been rather dull at Cousin Olivia's. Lilly was a good deal with her own friends, and Mrs Page with hers; and there never seemed any special place where they might sit, or anything in particular for them to do.

Louisa's home was at some distance from Mr Page's, and in a less fashionable street. It looked pleasant and cosy as the girls opened the gate. There was a small garden in front with gay flowerbeds; and on the piazza, which was shaded with vines, sat Mrs Agnew, with a little work-table by her side. She was a pretty and youthful-looking woman, and her voice and smile made them feel at home immediately.

'There is no need of anybody to introduce you,' she said. 'Lulu has described you so often that I know perfectly well which is Katy and which Clover. I am so glad you could come! Won't you go right in my bedroom by that long window and take off your things? Lulu has explained to you that I am lame and never walk, so you won't think it strange that I do not show you the way. She will be here in a moment. She ran upstairs to fetch the baby.'

The girls went into the bedroom. It was a pretty and unusual-looking apartment. The furniture was simple as could be, but bed and toilet and windows were curtained and frilled with white, and the walls were covered thick with pictures, photographs, and pen-and-ink sketches, and water-colour drawings, unframed, most of them, and just pinned up without regularity, so as to give each the best possible light. It was an odd way of arranging pictures; but Katy liked it, and would gladly have lingered to look at each one, only that she feared Mrs Agnew would expect them and would think it strange that they did not come back.

Just as they went out again to the piazza, Louisa came running downstairs with her little sister in her arms.

'I was curling her hair,' she explained, 'and did not hear you come in. Daisy, give Katy a kiss. Now another for Clover. Isn't she a darling?' embracing the child rapturously herself; 'now isn't she a little beauty?'

'Perfectly lovely!' cried the others, and soon all three were seated on the floor of the piazza, with Daisy in the midst, passing her from hand to hand, as if she had been something good to eat. She was used to it, and submitted with perfect good nature to being kissed, trotted, carried up and down, and generally made love to. Mrs Agnew sat by and laughed at the spectacle. When Baby was taken off for her noonday nap, Louisa took the girls into the parlour, another odd and pretty room, full of prints and sketches, and pictures of all sorts, some with frames, others with a knot of autumn leaves or a twist of ivy around them by way of a finish. There was a bowl of beautiful autumn roses on the table; and, though the price of one of Mrs Page's damask curtains would probably have bought the whole furniture of the room, everything was so bright, and homelike and pleasant-looking, that Katy's heart warmed at the sight. They were examining a portrait of Louisa with Daisy in her lap, painted by her father, when Mr Agnew came in. The girls liked his face at once. It was fine and frank; and nothing could be prettier than to see him pick up his invalid wife as if she had been a child, and carry her into the dining-room to her place at the head of the table.

Katy and Clover agreed afterward that it was the merriest dinner they had had since they left home. Mr Agnew told stories about painters and painting, and was delightful. No less so was the nice gossip upstairs in Louisa's room which followed dinner, or the afternoon frolic with Daisy, or the long evening spent in looking over books and photographs. Altogether the day seemed only too short. As they went out of the gate at ten o'clock, Mr Agnew following, lo! a dark figure emerged from behind a tree and joined Clover. It was Clarence!

'I thought I'd just walk this way,' he explained, 'the house has been dreadfully dull all day without you.'

Clover was immensely flattered, but Mrs Page's astonishment next day knew no bounds.

'Really,' she said, 'I have hopes of Clarence at last. I never knew him volunteer to escort anybody anywhere before in his life.'

'I say,' remarked Clarence, the evening before the girls went back to school, 'I say, suppose you write to a fellow sometimes, Clover?'

'Do you mean yourself by "a fellow"?' laughed Clover.

'You don't suppose I meant George Hickman, or that donkey of an Eels, did you?' retorted Clarence.

'No, I didn't. Well, I've no objection to writing to a fellow, if that fellow is you, provided the fellow answers my letters. Will you?'

'Yes,' gruffly, 'but you mustn't show 'em to any girls, or laugh at my writing, or I'll stop. Lilly says my writing is like beetle-tracks. Little she knows about it, though! I don't write to her. Promise, Clover!'

'Yes, I promise,' said Clover, pleased at the notion of Clare's proposing a correspondence of his own accord.

Next morning they all left for Hillsover. Clarence's friendship, and the remembrance of their day with the Agnews, were the pleasantest things that the girls carried away with them from their autumn vacation.

CHAPTER
10

A BUDGET OF LETTERS

'DEAREST ELSIE, – I didn't write you last Saturday, because that was the day we came back to school, and there hasn't been one minute since when I could. We thought, perhaps, Miss Jane would let us off from the abstracts on Sunday, because it was the first day, and school was hardly begun; and if she had, I was going to write to you instead; but she didn't. She said the only way to keep girls out of mischief was to keep them busy. Rose Red is sure that something has gone wrong with Miss Jane's missionary during the vacation – she's so dreadfully cross. Oh, dear, how I do hate to come back and be scolded by her again!

'I forget if I told you about the abstracts. They are of the sermons on Sunday, you know; and we have to give the texts, and the heads, and as much as we can remember of the rest. Sometimes Dr Prince begins, "I shall divide my subject into three parts," and tells what they are going to be. When he does that, most of the girls take out their pencils and put them down, and then they don't listen any more. Katy and I don't, for she says it isn't right to act in that way. Miss Jane pretends that she reads all the abstracts through, but she doesn't; for once, Rose Red, just to try her, wrote in the middle of hers, "I am sitting by my window at this moment, and a red cow is going down the street. I wonder if she is any relation to Mrs Seccomb's cow?" and Miss Jane never noticed it, but marked her "perfect" all the same. Wasn't it funny?

'But I must tell you about our journey back. Mr Page came all the way with us, and was ever so nice. Clarence rode down in the carriage to the depot. He gave me a real pretty india-rubber and gold pencil for a good-bye present. I think you and Dorry would like Clarence, only just at first you might say he was rather rude and cross. I did; but now I like him ever so much. Cousin Olivia gave Katy a worked collar and sleeves, and me an embroidered pocket-handkerchief with clover leaves in the corner. Wasn't it kind? I'm sorry I said in my last letter that we didn't enjoy our vacation. We didn't much; but it wasn't exactly Cousin Olivia's fault. She meant we should, but she didn't know how. Some people don't, you know. And don't tell any one I said so, will you?

'Rose Red got into the train before we did. She was so glad when we came that she cried. It was because she was home-sick waiting four hours at the Nunnery without us, she said. Rose is such a darling! She had a splendid vacation, and went to three parties and a picnic. Isn't it queer? – her winter bonnet is black velvet trimmed with pink, and so is mine. I wanted blue at first, but Cousin Olivia said pink was more stylish; and now I am glad, because I like to be like Rose.

'Katy and I have got No. 2 this term. It's a great deal pleasanter than our old room, and the entry-stove is just outside the door, so we shall keep warm. There is sun, too, only Mrs Nipson has nailed thick cotton over all the window except a little place at the top. Every window in the house is just so. You can't think how mad the girls are about it. The first night we had an indignation meeting, and passed resolutions, and some of the girls said they wouldn't stay – they should write to their fathers to come and take them home. None of them did, though. It's perfectly forlorn, not being able to look out. Oh, dear, how I wish it were spring!

'We've got a new dining-room. It's a great deal bigger than the old one, so now we all eat together, and don't have any first and second tables. It's ever so much nicer, for I used to get so dreadfully hungry waiting that I didn't know what to do. One thing is horrid, though; and that is, that every girl has to make a remark in French every day at dinner. The remarks are about a subject. Mrs Nipson gives out the subjects. Today the subject was "Les oiseaux", and Rose Red said, "J'aime beaucoup les oiseaux, especialement ceux qui sont rôtis," which made us all laugh. That ridiculous little Bella Arkwright said, "J'aime beaucoup les oiseaux qui sing." She thought sing was French! Every girl in the school began, "J'aime beaucoup les oiseaux"! Tomorrow the subject is "Jules César". I'm sure I don't know what to say. There isn't a word in Ollendorf about him.

'There are not so many new scholars this term as there were last. The girls think it is because Mrs Nipson isn't so popular as Mrs Florence used to be. Two or three of the new ones look pleasant, but I don't know them yet. Louisa Agnew is the nicest girl here next to Rose. Lilly Page says she is vulgar, because her father paints portraits, and they don't know the same people that Cousin Olivia knows; but she isn't a bit. We went to spend the day there just before we left Ashburn, and her father and mother are splendid. Their house is just full of all sorts of queer, interesting things, and pictures; and Mr Agnew told us ever so many stories about painters, and what they did. One was about a boy who used to make figures of lions in butter, and afterward he became famous. I forget his name. We had a lovely time. I wish you could see Lou's little sister Daisy. She's only two, and a perfect little beauty. She has got ten teeth, and hardly ever cries.

'Please ask papa – '

Just as Clover had got to this point, she was interrupted by Katy, who walked in with her hat on, and a whole handful of letters.

'See here!' she cried. 'Isn't this delightful? Miss Marsh took me with her to the post office, and we found these. Three for you, and two for me, and one for Rose. Wait a minute till I give Rose hers, and we'll read them together.'

In another moment the two were cosily seated, with their heads close together, opening their budget. First came one from papa.

'MY DEAR DAUGHTERS,

'It's for you, too, you see,' said Katy.

'Last week came your letter of the 31st, and we were glad to hear that you were well, and ready to go back to school. By the time this reaches you, you will be in Hillsover, and your winter term begun. Make the most of it, for we all feel as if we could never let you go from home again. Johnnie says she shall rub Spalding's Prepared Glue all over your dresses when you come back, so that you cannot stir. I am a little of the same way of thinking myself. Cecy has returned from boarding-school, and set up as a young lady. Elsie is much excited over the party dresses which Mrs Hall is having made for her, and goes over every day to see if anything new has come. I am glad, on this account, that you are away just now; for it would not be easy to keep steady heads and continue your studies, with so much going on next door. I have sent Cousin Olivia a cheque to pay for the things she bought for you, and am much obliged to her for seeing that you were properly fitted out. Katy was very right to consider expense, but I wish you to have all things needful. I enclose two ten-dollar bills, one for each of you, for pocket-money; and, with much love from the children, am,

'Yours affectionately,

'P. CARR

'PS – Cousin Helen has had a sharp attack, but is better.'

'I wish papa would write longer letters,' said Katy. 'He always sends us money, but he don't send half enough words with it.' She folded the letter, and fondled it affectionately.

'He's always so busy,' replied Clover. 'Don't you remember how he used to sit down at his desk, and scribble off his letters; and how somebody always was sure to ring the bell before he got through? I'm very glad to have some money, for now I can pay the sixty-two cents I owe you. It's my turn to read. This is from Elsie, and a real long one. Put away the bills first, Katy, or they'll be lost. That's right; now we'll begin together.'

'DEAR CLOVER – You don't know how glad I am when my turn comes to get a letter all to myself. Of course I read papa's, and all the rest you write to the family; but it never seems as if you were talking to me unless you begin, "Dear Elsie". I wish some time you'd put in a little note marked "private", just for me, which nobody else need see. It would be such fun! Please do. I should think you would have hated staying at Cousin Olivia's. When I read what she said about your travelling-dresses looking as if they had come out of the ark, I was just as mad as fire. But I shouldn't think you'd want much to go back to school either, though sometimes it must be splendid. John has named her old stockinet doll, which she used to call "Scratch-face", "Nippy", after Mrs Nipson; and I made her a muslin cap, and Dorry drew a pair of black spectacles round her eyes. She is a perfect fright, and John plays all the time that dreadful things happen to her. She pricks her with pins, and pretends she has the ear-ache, and lets her tumble down and hurt herself, till sometimes I nearly feel sorry, though it's all make-believe. When you wrote us about only having pudding for dinner, I didn't a bit. John put her into the rag-closet that very day, and has been starving her to death ever since; and Phil says it serves her right. You can't think how awfully lonely I sometimes get without you. If it wasn't for Helen Gibbs, that new girl I told you about, I shouldn't know what to do. She is the prettiest girl in Miss McCrane's school. Her hair curls just like mine, only it is four times as long, and a million times as thick; and her waist is really and truly not much bigger round than a bed-post. We're the greatest friends. She says she loves me just exactly as much as if I was her sister, but she never had any real sisters. She was quite mad the other day because I said I couldn't love her quite so well as you and Katy; and all recess-time she wouldn't speak to me, but now we've made up. Dorry is so awfully in love with her, that I never can get him to come into the room when she is here, and he blushes when we tease him about her. But this is a great secret. Dorry and I play chess every evening. He almost always beats, unless papa comes behind and helps me. Phil has learned, too, because he always wants to do everything that we do. Dorry gives him a castle, and a bishop, and a knight, and four pawns, and then beats him in six moves. Phil gets so mad that we can't help laughing. Last night he buttoned his king up inside his jacket, and said, "There! you can't checkmate me now any way!"

'Cecy has come home. She is a young lady now. She does her hair up quite different, and wears long dresses. This winter she is going to parties, and Mrs Hall is going to have a party for her on Thursday, with real, grown-up young ladies and gentlemen at it. Cecy has got some beautiful new dresses – a white muslin, a blue tarlatan, and a pink silk. The pink silk is the prettiest, I think. Cecy is real kind, and lets me see all her things. She has got a lovely breast-pin, too, and a new fan with ivory sticks, and all sorts of things. I wish I was grown-up. It must be so nice. I want to tell you something, only you mustn't tell anybody except Katy. Don't you remember how Cecy used to say that she never was going out to drive with young gentlemen, but was going to stay at home and read the Bible to poor people? Well, she didn't tell the truth; for she has been out three times already with Sylvester Slack in his buggy. When I told her she ought not to do so, because it was breaking a promise, she only laughed, and said I was a silly girl. Isn't it queer?

'I want to tell you what an awful thing I did the other night. Maria Avery invited me to tea, and papa said I might go. I didn't want to much, but I didn't know what to tell Maria, so I went. You know how poor they are, and how Aunt Lizzie used to say that they were "touchy", so I thought I would take great care not to hurry home right after tea, for fear they would think I was not enjoying myself. So I waited, and waited, and waited, and got so sleepy that I had to pinch my fingers to keep awake. At last I was sure that it might be almost nine, so I asked Mr Avery if he'd please take me home; and don't you believe, when we got there, it was a quarter past ten, and papa was just coming for me! Dorry said he guessed I must be enjoying myself to stay so late. I didn't tell anybody about it for three days, because I knew they'd laugh at me, and they did. Wasn't it funny? And old Mrs Avery looked as sleepy as I felt, and kept yawning behind her hand. I told papa if I had a watch of my own I shouldn't make such mistakes, and he laughed and said, "We'll see." Oh, do you suppose that means that he's going to give me one?

'We are so proud of Dorry's having taken two prizes at the examination yesterday. He took the second Latin prize, and the first mathematics. Dr Pullman says he thinks Dorry is one of the most thorough boys he ever saw. Isn't that nice? The prizes were books; one was the life of Benjamin Franklin, and the other the life of General Butler. Papa says he doesn't think much of the life of Butler; but Dorry has begun it, and says it is splendid. Phil says when he takes a prize he wants candy and a new knife; but he'll have to wait a good while unless he studies harder than he does now. He has just come in to tease me to go up into the garret and help him to get down his sledge, because he thinks it is going to snow; but there isn't a sign of it, and the weather is quite warm. I asked him what I should say for him to you, and he said, "Oh, tell her to come home, and anything you please!" I said, "Shall I give her your love, and say that you are very well?" and he says, "Oh, yes, Miss Elsie, I guess you'd think yourself mighty well if your head ached as much as mine does every day!" Don't be frightened, however, for he's just as fat and rosy as can be; but almost every day he says he feels sick about school-time. When papa was at Moorfield, Miss Finch believed him, and let him stay at home two mornings. I don't wonder at it, for you can think what a face he makes up; but he got well so fast that she pays no attention to him now. The other day, about eleven o'clock, papa met him coming along the road, shying stones at the birds, and making lots of noise. He told papa he felt so sick that his teacher had let him go home; but papa noticed that his mouth looked sticky, so he opened his dinner-basket, and found that the little scamp had eaten up all his dinner on the road, corned beef, bread and butter, a great piece of mince pie, and six pears. Papa couldn't help laughing, but he made him turn round and go right back to school again.

'I told you, in my last, about Johnnie's going to school with me now. She is very proud of it, and is always talking abou

"Elsie's and my school". She is twice as smart as the other little girls of her age. Miss McCrane has put her into the composition class, where they write compositions on their slates. The first subject was, "A Kitten"; and John's began, "She's a dear, little, soft, scratching thing, only you'd better not pull her by the tail, but she's real cunning." All the girls laughed, and Johnnie called out, "Well, it's true, anyhow."

'I can't write any more, for I must study my Latin. Besides, this is the longest letter that ever was. I have been four days writing it. Please send me one just as long. Old Mary and the children send lots of love, and papa says, "Tell Katy, if a pudding diet sets her to growing again, she must come home at once, for he couldn't afford it." Oh, dear, how I wish I could see you! Please give my love to Rose Red. She must be perfectly splendid.

> 'Your affectionate,
> 'ELSIE.'

'Oh, the dear little duck! Isn't that just like her?' said Clover. 'I think Elsie has a real genius for writing, don't you? She tells all the little things, and is so droll and cunning. Nobody writes such nice letters. Who's that from, Katy?'

'Cousin Helen, and it's been such a long time coming. Just look at this date! September 22nd – a whole month ago!' Then she began to read.

'DEAR KATY,

'It seems a long time since we have had a talk, but I've been less well lately, so that it has been difficult to write. Yesterday, I sat up for the first time in several weeks; and today I am dressed and beginning to feel like myself. I wish you could see my room this morning – I often wish this – but it is so particularly pretty, for little Helen has been in with a great basket full of leaves and flowers, and together we have dressed it to perfection. There are four vases of roses, a bowl full of chrysanthemums, and red leaves round all my pictures. The leaves are Virginia creeper. It doesn't last long, but is lovely while it lasts. Helen also brought a bird's nest which the gardener found in a hawthorn-tree on the lawn. It hangs on a branch, and she has tied it to one side of my bookshelves. On the opposite side is another nest quite different – a great, grey hornet's nest, as big as a band-box, which came from the mountains a year ago. I wondered if any such grow in the woods about Hillsover. In spite of the red leaves, the day is warm as summer, and the windows stand wide open. I suppose it is cooler with you, but I know it is delicious cold. Now that I think of it, you must be in Ashburn by this time. I hope you will enjoy every moment of your vacation.

'*Oct*. 19*th* – I did not finish my letter the day it was begun, dear Katy, and next morning it proved that I was not so strong as I fancied, and I had to go to bed again. I am still there, and, as you see, writing with a pencil; but do not be worried about me, for the doctor says I am mending, and soon I hope to be up and in my chair. The red leaves are gone, but the roses are lovely as ever, for little Helen keeps bringing me fresh ones. She has just been in to read me her composition. The subject was "Stars", and you can't think how much she found to say about them. She is a bright little creature, and it is a great pleasure to teach her. I am hardly ever so sick that she cannot come for her lessons, and she gets on fast. We have made an arrangement that when she knows more than I do, she is to give me lessons, and I am not sure that the time is so very far off.

'I must tell you about my Ben. He is a new canary which was given me in the summer, and lately he has grown so delightfully tame that I feel as if it were not a bird at all, but a fairy prince come to live with me and amuse me. The cage door is left open always now, and he flies in and out as he likes. He is a restless, inquisitive fellow, and visits any part of the room, trying each fresh thing with his bill to see if it is good to eat, and then perching on it to see if it is good to sit upon. He mistakes his own reflection in the looking-glass for another canary, and sits on the pincushion twittering and making love to himself for half an hour at a time. To watch him is one of my greatest amusements, especially just now when I am in bed so much. Sometimes he hides and keeps so still that I have not the least idea where he is. But the moment I call, ''Ben, Ben'', and hold out my finger, wings begin to rustle, and out he flies and perches on my finger. He isn't the least bit in the world afraid, but sits on my head or shoulder, eats out of my mouth, and kisses me with his beak. He is on the pillow at this moment making runs at my pencil, of which he is mortally jealous. It is just so with my combs and brushes, if I attempt to do my hair; he cannot bear to have me do anything but play with him. I do wish I could show him to you and Clover.

'Little Helen, my other pet, has just come in with a sponge cake which she frosted herself. She sends her love, and says when you come to see me next summer she will frost you each one just like it. Good-bye, my Katy. I had nothing to write about, and have written it; but I never like to keep silent too long, or let you feel as if you were forgotten by your loving cousin,

'HELEN

'P.S. – Be sure to wear plenty of warm wraps for your winter walks. And, Katy dear, you must eat meat every day. Mrs Nipson will probably give up her favourite puddings now that the cold weather has begun; but, if not, write to papa.'

'Isn't that letter Cousin Helen all over?' said Katy. 'So

little about her illness, and so bright and merry, and yet she has really been sick. Papa says "a sharp attack". Isn't she the dearest person in the world, next to papa, I mean?'

'Yes, indeed. There's nobody like her. I do hope we can go to see her next summer. Now it's my turn. I can't think who this letter is from. Oh, Clarence! Katy, I can't let you see this. I promised Clare that I wouldn't show his letters to anybody, not even you.'

'Oh very well. But you've got another. Dorry, isn't it? Read that first, and I'll go away and leave you in peace.'

So Clover read:

'DEAR CLOVER – Elsie says she is going to write to you today, but I won't stop, because next Saturday I'm going out fishing with the Slacks. There are a great many trout now in Blue Brook. Eugene caught six the other day – no, five, one was a minnow. Papa has given me a splendid rod; it lets out as tall as a house. I hope I shall catch with it. Alexander says the trout will admire it so much that they can't help biting; but he was only funning. Elsie and I play chess most every night. She plays a real good game for a girl. Sometimes pa helps, and then she beats. Miss Finch is well. She don't keep house quite like Katy did, and I don't like her so well as I do you; but she's pretty nice. The other day we had a nutting picnic, and she gave me and Phil a loaf of Election cake and six quince turnovers to carry. The boys gave three cheers for her when they saw them. Did Elsie tell you that I have invented a new machine? It is called "The Intellectual Peach Parer". There is a place to hold a book while you pare the peaches. It is very convenient. I don't think of anything else to tell you. Cecy has got home, and is going to have a party next week. She's grown up now, she says, and she wears her hair quite different. It's a great deal thicker than it used to be. Elsie says it's because there are rats in it; but I don't believe her. Elsie has got a new friend. Her name is Helen Gibbs. She's quite pretty.

'Your affectionate brother,
'DORRY'

'PS – John wants to put in a note.'

John's note was written in a round hand, as easy to read as print.

'DEAR CLOVER – I am well, and hope you are the same. I wish you would write me a letter of my own. I go to school with Elsie now. We write compossizions. They are hard to write. We don't go up into the loft half so much as we used to when you ware at home. Mrs Worrett came to dinner last week. She says she ways two hundred and atey pounds. I should think it would be dredful to way that. I only way 76. My head comes up to the mark on the door where you ware mesured when you ware twelve – isn't that tal? Good-bye. I send a kiss to Katy.

'Your loving,
'JOHN'

After they had finished this note, Katy went away, leaving Clover to open Clarence's letter by herself. It was not so well written or spelt as Dorry's by any means.

'DEAR CLOVER – Don't forget what you promised. I mene about not showing this. And don't tell Lilly I rote. If you do, she'll be as mad as hops. I haven't been doing much since you went away. School begun yesterday, and I am glad; for it's awfully dull now that you girls have gone. Mother says Guest has got flees on him, so she won't let him come into the house any more. I stay out in the barn with him insted. He is well, and sends you a wag of his tail. Jim and me are making him a collar. It is black, with G. P. on it, for Guest Page, you know. A lot of boys had a camping out last week. I went. It was really jolly; but ma wouldn't let me stay all night, so I lost the best part. They rosted scullpins for supper, and had a bonfire. The camp was on Harstnet Hill. Next time you come I'll take you out there. Pa has gone to Mane on bizness. He said I must take care of the house, so I've borrowed Jim's gun, and if any robers come I mean to shoot them. I always go to sleep with a broom agenst the door, so as to wake up when they open it. This morning I thought they had come, for the broom was gone, and the gun, too; but it was only Briget. She opened the door, and it fell down; but I didn't wake up, so she took it away, and put the gun in the closset. I was mad, I can tell you.

'This is only a short letter, but I hope you will answer it soon. Give my love to Katy, and tell Dorry that if he likes I'll send him my compas for his machenery, because I've got two.

'Your affectionate Cousin,
'CLARENCE PAGE'

This was the last of the budget. As Clover folded it up, she was dismayed by the tinkle of the tea-bell.

'Oh, dear!' she cried, 'there's tea, and I have not finished my letter to Elsie. Where has the afternoon gone? How splendid it has been! I wish I could have four letters every day as long as I live.'

CHAPTER
11

CHRISTMAS BOXES

October was a delightful month, clear and sparkling; but early in November the weather changed, and became very cold. Thick frosts fell, every leaf vanished from the woods, in the gardens only blackened stalks remained to show where once the summer flowers had been. In spite of the stove outside the door, No. 2 began to be chilly. More than once Katy found her tooth-brush stiff with ice in the morning. It was a foretaste of what winter was to be, and the girls shivered at the prospect.

Toward the end of November Miss Jane caught a heavy cold. Unsparing of herself as of others, she went on hearing her classes as usual; and nobody paid much attention to her hoarseness and flushed cheeks, until she grew so much worse that she was forced to go to bed. There she stayed for nearly four weeks. It made a great change in the school, and the girls found it such a relief to have her sharp voice and eyes taken away, that I am afraid they were rather glad of her illness than otherwise.

Katy shared in this feeling of relief. She did not like

Miss Jane; it was pleasant not to have to see or hear of her. But as day after day passed, and still she continued ill, Katy's conscience began to prick. One night she lay awake a long time, and heard Miss Jane coughing violently. Katy feared she was very sick, and wondered who took care of her all night and all day. None of the girls went near her. The servants were always busy. And Mrs Nipson, who did not love Miss Jane, was busy too.

In the morning, while studying and practising, Katy caught herself thinking over this question. At last she asked Miss Marsh –

'How is Miss Jane today?'

'About the same. She is not dangerously ill, the doctor says; but she coughs a great deal, and has some fever.'

'Is anybody sitting with her?'

'Oh, no! there is no need of anyone. Susan answers the bell, and she has her medicine on the table within reach.'

It sounded forlorn enough. Katy had lived in a sick-room so long herself that she knew just how dreary it is for an invalid to be left alone with 'medicine within reach', and someone to answer a bell. She began to feel sorry for Miss Jane, and almost without intending it went down to the entry, and tapped at her door. The 'Come in!' sounded very faint; and Miss Jane as she lay in bed looked weak and dismal, and quite unlike the sharp, terrible person whom the girls feared so much. She was amazed at the sight of Katy, and made a feeble attempt to hold up her head and speak as usual.

'What is it, Miss Carr?'

'I only came to see how you are,' said Katy, abashed at her own daring, 'you coughed so much last night that

I was afraid you were worse. Isn't there something I
could do for you?'

'Thank you,' said Miss Jane, 'you are very kind.'

Think of Miss Jane's thanking anybody, and calling
anybody kind!

'I should be very glad. Isn't there anything?' repeated
Katy, encouraged.

'Well, I don't know; you might put another stick of
wood on the fire,' said Miss Jane, in an ungracious tone.

Katy did so; and seeing that the iron cup on top of the
stove was empty, she poured some water into it. Then
she took a look about the room. Books and papers were
scattered over the table; clean clothes from the wash lay
on the chairs; nothing was in its place; and Katy, who
knew how particular Miss Jane was on the subject of
order, guessed at the discomfort which this untidy state
of affairs must have caused her.

'Wouldn't you like to have me put these away?' she
asked, touching the pile of clothes.

Miss Jane sighed impatiently, but she did not say no; so
Katy, taking silence for consent, opened the drawers,
and laid the clothes inside, guessing at the right places
with a sort of instinct, and making as little noise and
bustle as possible. Next she moved quietly to the table,
where she sorted and arranged the papers, piled up the
books, and put the pens and pencils in a small tray which
stood there for the purpose. Lastly, she began to dust the
table with her pocket-handkerchief, which proceeding
roused Miss Jane at once.

'Don't,' she said, 'there is a duster in the cupboard.'

Katy could not help smiling; but she found the duster,
and proceeded to put the rest of the room into nice

order, laying a fresh towel over the bedside table, and arranging watch, medicine, and spoon within reach. Miss Jane lay and watched her. I think she was as much surprised at herself for permitting all this as Katy was at being permitted to do it. Sick people often consent because they feel too weak to object. After all, it was comfortable to have some one come in and straighten the things which for ten days past had vexed her neat eyes with their untidiness.

Lastly, smoothing the quilt, Katy asked if Miss Jane wouldn't like to have her pillow shaken up?

'I don't care,' was the answer.

It sounded discouraging; but Katy boldly seized the pillow, beat, smoothed, and put it again in place. Then she went out of the room as noiselessly as she could, Miss Jane never saying, 'Thank you', or seeming to observe whether she went or stayed.

Rose Red and Clover could hardly believe their ears when told where she had been. They stared at her as people stare at Van Amburgh when he comes safely out of the lion's den.

'My stars!' exclaimed Rose, drawing a long breath. 'You didn't really? And she hasn't bitten your head off!'

'Not a bit,' said Katy, laughing. 'What's more, I'm going again.'

She was as good as her word. After that she went to see Miss Jane very often. Almost always there was some little thing which she could do – the fire needed mending, or the pitcher to be filled with ice-water, or Miss Jane wanted the blinds opened or shut. Gradually she grew used to seeing Katy about the room. One morning she actually allowed her to brush her hair; and Katy's touch was so light and pleasant that afterwards Miss Jane begged her to do it every day.

'What makes you such a good nurse?' she asked one afternoon rather abruptly.

'Being sick myself,' replied Katy, gently.

Then, in answer to further questioning, she told of her four years' illness, and her life upstairs, keeping house and studying lessons all alone by herself. Miss Jane did not say anything when she got through; but Katy fancied that she looked at her in a new and kinder way.

So time went on till Christmas. It fell on a Friday that year, which shortened the holidays by a day, and disappointed many of the girls. Only a few went home, the rest were left to pass the time as best they might till Monday, when lessons were to begin again.

'It isn't much like merry Christmas,' sighed Clover to herself, as she looked up at the uncottoned space at the top of the window, and saw great snowflakes wildly whirling by. No. 2 felt cold and dreary, and she was glad to exchange it for the schoolroom, round whose warm stove a cluster of girls was huddling. Everybody was in bad spirits; there was a tendency to talk about home, and the nice time which people were having there, and the very bad time they themselves were having at the Nunnery.

'Isn't it mis-e-ra-ble? I shall cry all night, I know I shall, I am so homesick,' gulped Lilly, who had taken possession of her room-mate's shoulder and was weeping ostentatiously.

'I declare, you're just Mrs Gummidge in "David Copperfield" over again,' said Rose. 'You recollect her, girls, don't you? When the porridge was burnt, you know – "All of us felt the disappointment, but Mrs Gummidge felt it the most." Isn't Lilly a real Mrs Gummidge, girls?'

This observation changed Lilly's tears into anger. 'You're as hateful and as horrid as you can be, Rose Red!' she exclaimed, angrily. Then she flew out of the room, and shut the door behind her with a bang.

'There! she's gone upstairs cross,' said Louisa Agnew.

'I don't care if she has,' replied Rose, who was in a perverse mood.

'I wish you hadn't said that, Rosy,' whispered Clover. 'Lilly really felt badly.'

'Well, what if she did? So do I feel badly, and you, and the rest of us. Lilly hasn't taken out a patent for bad feelings, which nobody must infringe. What business has she to make us feel badder by setting up to be so much worse off than the rest of the world?'

Clover said nothing, but went on with a book she was reading. In less than ten minutes, Rose, whose sun seldom stayed long behind a cloud, was at her elbow, dimpling and coaxing.

'I forgive you,' she whispered, giving Clover's arm a little pinch.

'What for?'

'For being in the right. About Lilly, I mean. I was rather hateful to her, I confess. Never mind. When she comes downstairs, I'll make up for it. She's a crocodile, if ever there was one; but, as she's your cousin, I'll be good to her. Kiss me quick to prove that you're not vexed.'

'Vexed, indeed!' said Clover, kissing the middle of the

pink cheek. 'I wonder if anybody ever stayed vexed with you for ten minutes together, you Rosy-Posy you!'

'Bless you, yes! Miss Jane, for example. She hates me like poison, and all the time. Well, what of it? I know she's sick, but I "can't tell a lie, pa", on that account. Where's Katy?'

'Gone in to see her, I believe.'

'One of these days,' prophesied Rose, solemnly, 'she'll go into that room, and she'll never come out again! Miss Jane is getting back into biting condition. I advise Katy to be careful. What's that noise? Sleigh-bells, I declare! Girls' – mounting a desk, and peeping out of the window – 'somebody's got a big box – a big one! Here's old Joyce at the door, with his sledge. Now whose do you suppose it is?'

'It's for me! I'm sure it's for me!' cried half a dozen voices.

'Bella, my love, peep over the balusters, and see if you can't see the name,' cried Louisa; and Bella, nothing loth, departed at once on this congenial errand.

'No, I can't,' she reported, coming back from the hall. 'The name's tipped up against the wall. There's two boxes! One is big, and one is little!'

'Oh, who can they be for?' clamoured the girls. Half the school expected boxes, and had been watching the storm all day, with a dreadful fear that it would block the roads, and delay the expected treasures.

At this moment Mrs Nipson came in.

'There will be the usual study hour this evening,' she announced. 'All of you will prepare lessons for Monday morning. Miss Carr, come here for a moment, if you please.'

Clover, wondering, followed her into the entry.

'A parcel has arrived for you, and a box,' said Mrs Nipson. 'I presume that they contain articles for Christmas. I will have the nails removed, and both of them placed in your room this evening, but I expect you to refrain from examining them until tomorrow. The vacation does not open until after study-hour tonight, and it will then be too late for you to begin.'

'Very well, ma'am,' said Clover, demurely. But the minute Mrs Nipson's back was turned, she gave a jump, and rushed into the schoolroom.

'O girls,' she cried, 'what do you think? Both the boxes are for Katy and me.'

'Both!' cried a disappointed chorus.

'Yes, both. Mrs Nipson said so. I'm so sorry for you. But isn't it nice for us? We never had a box from home before, you know; and I didn't think we should, it's so far off. It's too lovely! But I do hope yours will come tonight.'

Clover's voice was so sympathizing, for all its glee, that nobody could help being glad with her.

'You little darling!' said Louisa, giving her a hug. 'I'm rejoiced that the box is yours. The rest of us are always getting them, and you and Katy never had a thing before. I hope it's a nice one!'

'Oh, it's sure to be nice! It's from home, you know,' responded Clover, with a happy smile. Then she left the room to find Katy, and tell the wonderful news.

Study hour seemed unusually long that night. The minute it was over, the sisters ran to No. 2. There stood the boxes, a big wooden one, with all the nails taken out of the lid, and a smaller paper one, carefully tied up and sealed. It was almost more than the girls could do to obey orders and not peep.

'I feel something hard,' announced Clover, inserting a finger-tip under the lid.

'Oh, do you?' cried Katy. Then, making an heroic effort, she jumped into bed.

'It's the only way,' she said, 'you'd better come, too, Clovy. Blow the candle out, and let's get to sleep as fast as we can, so as to make morning come quicker.'

Katy dreamed of home that night. Perhaps it was that which made her wake so early. It was not five o'clock, and the room was perfectly dark. She did not like to disturb Clover, so she lay perfectly still, for hours as it seemed, till a faint grey dawn crept in, and revealed the outlines of the big box standing by the window. Then she could wait no longer, but crept out of bed, crossed the floor on tiptoe, and raising the lid a little put in her hand. Something crumby and sugary met it, and when she drew it out, there, fitting on her finger like a ring, was a round cake with a hole in the middle of it.

'Oh! it's one of Debby's jumbles!' she exclaimed.

'Where? What are you doing? Give me one too!' cried Clover, starting up. Katy rummaged till she found another, then, half frozen, she ran back to bed; and the two lay nibbling the jumbles, and talking about home, till dawn deepened into daylight, and morning was fairly come.

Breakfast was half an hour later than usual, which was comfortable. As soon as it was over, the girls proceeded to unpack their box. The day was so cold that they wrapped themselves in shawls, and Clover put on a hood and thick gloves. Rose Red, passing the door, burst out laughing, and recommended that she should add india-rubber boots and an umbrella.

'Oh, come in,' cried the sisters, 'come in, and help us open our box!'

'Oh, by the way, you have a box, haven't you?' said Rose, who was perfectly aware of the important fact, and had presented herself with the hope of being asked to look on. 'Thank you, but perhaps I would better come some other time. I shall be in your way.'

'You impostor!' said Clover, while Katy seized Rose and pulled her into the room. 'There, sit on the bed, you ridiculous goose, and put on my grey cloak. How can you be so absurd as to say you won't? You know we want you, and you know you came on purpose!'

'Did I? Well perhaps I did,' laughed Rose. Then Katy lifted off the lid, and set it against the door. It was an exciting moment.

'Just look here!' cried Katy.

The top of the box was mostly taken up with four square paper boxes, round which parcels of all shapes and sizes were wedged and fitted. The whole was a miracle of packing. It had taken Miss Finch three mornings, with assistance from old Mary, and much advice from Elsie, to do it so beautifully.

Each box held a different kind of cake. One was full of jumbles, another of ginger-snaps, a third of crullers, and the fourth contained a big square loaf of frosted plum-cake, with a circle of sugar almonds set in the frosting. How the trio exclaimed at this!

'I never imagined anything so nice,' declared Rose, with her mouth full of jumble. 'As for those snaps, they're simply perfect. What can be in all those fascinating bundles? Do hurry and open one, Katy.'

Dear little Elsie! The first two bundles opened were hers – a white hood for Katy, and a blue one for Clover, both of her own knitting, and so nicely done. The girls were enchanted.

'How she has improved!' said Katy. 'She knits better than either of us, Clover.'

'There never was such a clever little darling!' responded Clover; and they patted the hoods, tried them on before the glass, and spent so much time in admiring them that Rose grew impatient.

'I declare,' she cried, 'it isn't any of my funeral, I know, but if you don't open another parcel soon, I shall certainly fall to myself. It seems as if, what with cold and curiosity, I couldn't wait.'

'Very well,' said Katy, laying aside her hood, with one final glance. 'Take out a bundle, Clover. It's your turn.'

Clover's bundle was for herself, 'Evangeline' in blue and gold, and pretty soon the 'Golden Legend', in the same binding, appeared for Katy. Both these were from Dorry. Next came a couple of round packages of exactly the same size. These proved to be inkstands, covered with Russian leather – one marked, 'Katy, from Johnnie', and the other 'Clover, from Phil'. It was evident that the children had done their shopping together, for presently two long, narrow parcels revealed carved pen-handles, precisely alike; and these were labelled, 'Katy, from Phil', and 'Clover, from Johnnie'.

What fun it was opening those bundles! The girls made a long business of it, taking out but one at a time, exclaiming, admiring, and exhibiting to Rose, before they began upon another. They laughed, they joked, but I do not think it would have taken much to make either of them cry. It was almost too tender a pleasure – these proofs of loving remembrance from the little ones; and each separate article seemed full of the very look and feel of home.

'What can this be?' said Katy, as she unrolled a paper and disclosed a pretty round box. She opened. Nothing was visible but pink cotton wool. Katy peeped beneath, and gave a cry.

'Oh, Clovy! such a lovely thing! It's from papa – of course, it's from papa! How could he? It's a great deal too pretty.'

The 'lovely thing' was a long slender chain for Katy's watch, worked in fine yellow gold. Clover admired it extremely; and her joy knew no bounds when further search revealed another box with a precisely similar chain for herself. It was too much. The girls fairly cried with pleasure.

'There never was such a papa in the world,' they said.

'Yes, there is; mine is just as good,' declared Rose, twinkling away a little tear-drop from her own eyes. 'Now, don't cry, honeys. Your papa's an angel, there's no doubt about it. I never saw such pretty chains in my life – never. As for the children, they're little ducks. You certainly are a wonderful family. Katy, I'm dying to know what is in that blue parcel.'

The blue parcel was from Cecy, and contained a pretty blue ribbon for Clover. There was a pink one also, with a pink ribbon for Katy. Everybody had thought of the girls. Old Mary sent them each a yard measure; Miss Finch, a thread-case, stocked with differently coloured cottons. Alexander had cracked a bag full of hickory nuts.

'Did you ever?' said Rose, when this last was produced. 'What a thing it is to be popular! Mrs Hall! Who's Mrs Hall?' as Clover unwrapped a tiny carved easel.

'She's Cecy's mother,' explained Clover. 'Wasn't she kind to send me this, Katy? And here's Cecy's photograph in a little frame for you.'

Never was such a wonderful box. It appeared to have no bottom whatever. Under the presents were parcels of figs, prunes, almonds, raisins, candy; under those, apples and pears. There seemed no end to the surprises.

At last all were out.

'Now,' said Katy, 'let's throw back the apples and pears, and then I want you to help me divide the other things, and make up some packages for the girls. They are all so disappointed not to have their boxes. I should like to have them share ours. Wouldn't you, Clover?'

'Yes, indeed; I was just going to propose it.'

So Clover cut twenty-nine squares of white paper, Rose and Katy sorted and divided, and pretty soon ginger-snaps and almonds and sugar-plums were walking down all the entries, and a gladsome crunching showed that the girls had found pleasant employment. None of the snowed-up boxes got through till Monday, so except for Katy and Clover the school would have had no Christmas treat at all.

They carried Mrs Nipson a large slice of cake, and a basket full of the beautiful red apples. All the teachers were remembered, and the servants. The S.S.U.C. was convened and feasted; and as for Rose, Louisa, and other special cronies, dainties were heaped upon them with such unsparing hand that they finally remonstrated.

'You're giving everything away. You'll have none left for yourselves.'

'Yes, we shall – plenty,' said Clover. 'Oh, Rosy! here's such a splendid pear! You must have this.'

'No, no!' protested Rose; but Clover forced it into her pocket.

'The Carrs' Box' was always quoted in the Nunnery afterwards, as an example of what papas and mammas could accomplish, when they were of the right sort, and really wanted to make schoolgirls happy. Distributing their treasures kept Katy and Clover so busy that it was not until after dinner that they found time to open the smaller box. When they did so, they were sorry for the delay. The box was full of flowers – roses, geranium-leaves, heliotrope, beautiful red and white carnations, all so bedded in cotton that the frost had not touched them. But they looked chilled, and Katy hastened to put them in warm water, which she had been told was the best way to revive drooping flowers.

Cousin Helen had sent them; and underneath, sewed to the box, that they might not shake about and do mischief, were two flat parcels, wrapped in tissue paper, and tied with white ribbon, in Cousin Helen's dainty way. They were glove-cases, of quilted silk, delicately scented, one white, and one lilac; and to each was pinned a loving note, wishing the girls a Merry Christmas.

'How awfully good people are!' said Clover. 'I do think we ought to be the best girls in the world.'

Last of all, Katy made a choice little selection from her stores, a splendid apple, a couple of fine pears, a handful of raisins and figs, and, with a few of the freshest flowers in a wine-glass, she went down the Row and tapped at Miss Jane's door.

Miss Jane was sitting up for the first time, wrapped in a shawl, and looking very thin and pale. Katy, who had almost ceased to be afraid of her, went in cheerily.

'We've had a splendid box from home, Miss Jane, full of all sorts of things. It has been such fun unpacking it. I've brought an apple, and some pears, and this little bunch of flowers. Wasn't it a nice Christmas for us?'

'Yes,' said Miss Jane, 'very nice indeed. I heard some one saying in the entry that you had a box. Thank you,' as Katy set the basket and glass on the table. 'Those flowers are very sweet. I wish you a Merry Christmas, I'm sure.'

This was much from Miss Jane, who could not help speaking shortly, even when she was pleased. Katy withdrew in high glee.

But that night, just before bed-time, something happened so surprising that Katy, telling Clover about it afterward, said she half fancied that she must have dreamed it all. It was about eight o'clock in the evening: she was passing down Quaker Row, and Miss Jane called and asked her to come in. Miss Jane's cheeks were flushed, and she spoke fast, as if she had resolved to say something, and thought the sooner it was over the better.

'Miss Carr,' she began, 'I wish to tell you that I made up my mind some time since that we did you an injustice last term. It is not your attentions to me during my illness which have changed my opinion – that was done before I fell ill. It is your general conduct, and the good influence which I have seen you exert over other girls, which convinced me that we must have been wrong about you.

That is all. I thought you might like to hear me say this, and I shall say the same to Mrs Nipson.'

'Thank you,' said Katy, 'you don't know how glad I am!' She half thought she would kiss Miss Jane, but somehow it didn't seem possible; so she shook hands very heartily instead, and flew to her room, feeling as if her feet were wings.

'It seems too good to be true. I want to cry, I am so happy,' she told Clover. 'What a lovely day this has been!'

And of all that she had received, I think Katy considered this explanation with Miss Jane as her very best Christmas box.

12

WAITING FOR SPRING

School was a much happier place after this. Mrs Nipson never alluded to the matter, but her manner altered. Katy felt that she was no longer watched or distrusted, and her heart grew light.

In another week Miss Jane was so much better as to be hearing her classes again. Illness had not changed her materially. It is only in novels that rheumatic fever sweetens tempers, and makes disagreeable people over into agreeable ones. Most of the girls disliked her as much as ever. Her tongue was just as sharp, and her manner as grim. But for Katy, from that time forward, there was a difference. Miss Jane was not affectionate to her – it was not in her nature to be that – but she was civil and considerate, and, in a dry way, friendly; and gradually Katy grew to have an odd sort of liking for her.

Do any of you know how incredibly long winter seems in climates where for weeks together the thermometer stands at zero? There is something hopeless in such cold. You think of summer as of a thing read about somewhere in a book, but which has no actual existence. Winter seems the only reality in the world.

Katy and Clover felt this hopelessness growing upon them as the days went on, and the weather grew more and more severe. Ten, twenty, even thirty degrees below zero, was no unusual register for the Hillsover thermometers. Such cold half-frightened them, but nobody else was frightened or surprised. It was dry, brilliant cold. The December snows lay unmelted on the ground in March, and the paths cut then were crisp and hard still, only the white walls on either side had risen higher and higher, till only a moving line of hoods and tippets was visible above them, when the school went out for its daily walk. Morning after morning the girls woke to find thick crusts of frost on their window-panes, and every drop of water in wash-bowl or pitcher turned to solid ice. Night after night, Clover, who was a chilly little creature, lay shivering and unable to sleep, notwithstanding the hot bricks at her feet, and the many wraps which Katy piled upon her. To Katy herself the cold was more bracing than depressing. There was something in her blood which responded to the sharp tingle of frost, and she gained in strength in a remarkable way during this winter. But the long storms told upon her spirits. She pined for spring and home more than she liked to tell, and felt the need of variety in their monotonous life, where the creeping days appeared like weeks, and the weeks stretched themselves out, and seemed as long as months do in other places.

The girls resorted to all sorts of devices to keep themselves alive during this dreary season. They had little epidemics of occupation. At one time it was 'spattering', when all faces and fingers had a tendency to smudges of India ink; and there was hardly a fine comb or tooth-brush fit for use in the establishment. Then a rage for tatting set in, followed by a fever of fancy-work, every one falling in love with the same pattern at the same time, and copying and re-copying, till nobody could bear the sight of it. At one time Clover counted eighteen girls all at work on the same bead and canvas pincushion. Later there was a short period of *decalcomanie*; and then came the grand album craze, when thirty-three girls out of the thirty-nine sent for blank books bound in red morocco, and began to collect signatures and sentiments. Here, also, there was a tendency toward repetition.

Sally Austin added to her autograph these lines of her own composition:

> When on this page your beauteous eyes you bend,
> Let it remind you of your absent friend,
>
> SALLY J. AUSTIN
> Galveston, Texas

The girls found this sentiment charming, at least a dozen borrowed it, and in half the albums in the school you might read, 'When on this page your beauteous eyes,' etc. Esther Dearborn wrote in Clover's book: 'The better part of valour is discretion.' Why she wrote it nobody knew, or why it was more applicable to Clover than to any one; but the sentiment proved popular, and was repeated over and over again, above various neatly-written signatures. There was a strife as to who should display the largest collection. Some of the girls sent home for autographs of distinguished persons, which they pasted in their books. Rose Red, however, outdid them all.

'Did I ever show you mine?' she asked one day, when most of the girls were together in the schoolroom.

'No, never!' cried a number of voices. 'Have you got one? Oh, do let us see it!'

'Certainly, I'll get it right away, if you like,' said Rose, obligingly.

She went to her room, and returned with a shabby old blank book in her hand. Some of the girls looked disappointed.

'The cover of mine isn't very nice,' explained Rose. 'I'm going to have it re-bound one of these days. You see it's not a new album at all, nor a school album; but it's very valuable to me.' Here she heaved a sentimental sigh. 'All my friends have written in it,' she said.

The girls were quite impressed by the manner in which Rose said this. But, when they turned over the pages of the album, they were even more impressed. Rose had evidently been on intimate terms with a circle of most distinguished persons. Half the autographs in the book were from gentlemen, and they were dated all over the world.

'Just listen to this!' cried Louisa, and she read –

Thou may'st forget me, but never never shall I forget thee!

ALPHONSO OF CASTILE
THE ESCURIAL, April 1st

'Who's he?' asked a circle of awe-struck girls.

'Didn't you ever hear of him? Youngest brother of the King of Spain,' replied Rose, carelessly.

'Oh, my! and just hear this,' exclaimed Annie Silsbie –

If you ever deign to cast a thought in my direction,
Miss Rose remember me always as
Thy devoted servitor,
POTEMKIN MONTMORENCY
ST PETERSBURG, July 10th

'And this!' shrieked Alice White –

> They say love is a thorn. I say it is a dart,
> And yet I cannot tear thee from my heart.
>> ANTONIO, Count of Valambrosa

'Do you really and truly know a count?' asked Bella, backing away from Rose, with eyes as big as saucers.

'Know Antonio de Valambrosa? I should think I did,' replied Rose. 'Nobody in this country knows him so well, I fancy.'

'And he wrote that for you?'

'How else could it get into my book, goosey?'

This was unanswerable, and Rose was installed from that time forward in the minds of Bella and the rest as a heroine of the first water. Katy, however, knew better, and the first time she caught Rose alone she attacked her on the subject.

'Now, Rosy-Posy, confess. Who wrote all those absurd autographs in your book?'

'Absurd autographs! What do you mean?'

'All those counts and things. No, it's no use; you shan't wriggle away till you tell me.'

'Oh, Antonio and dear Potemkin, do you mean them?'

'Yes, of course I do.'

'And you really want to know?'

'Yes.'

'And will you swear not to tell?'

'Yes.'

'Well, then,' bursting into a laugh, 'I wrote every one of them myself.'

'Did you really? When?'

'Day before yesterday. I thought Lilly needed taking

down, she was so set up with her autographs of Wendell
Phillips and Mr Seward, so I just sat down and wrote a
book full. It only took me half an hour. I meant to write
some more; in fact, I had one all ready –

> I am dead, or pretty near:
> David's done for me I fear.

GOLIATH OF GATH;

but I was afraid even Bella wouldn't swallow that, so I
tore out the page. I'm sorry I did now, for I really think
the geese would have believed it. Written in his last
moments, you know, to oblige an ancestor of my own,'
added Rose, in a tone of explanation.

'You monkey!' cried Katy, highly diverted. But she
kept Rose's counsel, and I dare say some of the Hillsover
girls believe in that wonderful album to this day.

It was not long after that a sad piece of news came for
Bella. Her father was dead. Their home was in Sorra,
too far to allow of her returning for the funeral; so the
poor little girl stayed at school, to bear her trouble as
best she might. Katy, who was always kind to children,
and had somewhat affected Bella from the first on account of her resemblance to Elsie in height and figure,
was specially tender to her now, which Bella repaid with
the gift of her whole queer little heart. Her affectionate
demonstrations were rather of the monkey order, and
not infrequently troublesome; but Katy was never otherwise than patient and gentle with her, though Rose,
and even Clover, remonstrated on what they called this
'singular intimacy'.

'Poor little soul! it's so hard for her, and she's only
eleven years old,' she told them.

'She has such a funny way of looking at you sometimes,' said Rose, who was very observant. 'It is just the air of a squirrel who has hidden a nut, and doesn't want you to find out where, and yet can hardly help indicating it with his paw. She's got something on her mind, I'm sure.'

'Half a dozen things very likely,' added Clover; 'she's such a mischief.'

But none of them guessed what this 'something' was.

Early in January Mrs Nipson announced that in four weeks she proposed to give a 'soirée', to which all young ladies whose records were entirely free from marks during the intervening period would be allowed to come. This announcement created great excitement, and the school set itself to be good; but marks were easy to get, and gradually one girl after another lost her chance, till by the appointed day only a limited party descended to join the festivities, and nearly half the school was left upstairs to sigh over past sins. Katy and Rose were among the unlucky ones. Rose had incurred a mark by writing a note in study hour, and Katy by being five minutes late to dinner. They consoled themselves by dressing Clover's hair, and making her look as pretty as possible, and then stationed themselves in the upper hall at the head of the stairs to watch her career, and get as much fun out of the occasion as they could.

Pretty soon they saw Clover below on Professor Seccomb's arm. He was a kindly, pleasant man, with a bald head, and it was a fashion among the girls to admire him.

'Doesn't she look pretty?' said Rose. 'Just look at Mrs Searles, Katy. She's grinning at Clover like a Cheshire cat. What a wonderful cap that is of hers! She had it when Sylvia was here at school, eight years ago.'

'Hush! she'll hear you.'

'No, she won't! There's Ellen beginning her piece. I know she's frightened by the way she plays. Hark! how she hurries the time!'

'There! they're going to have refreshments, after all!' cried Esther Dearborn, as trays of lemonade and cake-baskets appeared below on their way to the parlour. 'Isn't it a shame to have to stay up here?'

'Professor Seccomb! Professor!' called Rose, in a daring whisper. 'Take pity upon us. We are starving for a piece of cake.'

The Professor gave a jump, then retreated, and looked upward. When he saw the circle of hungry faces peering down, he doubled up with laughter. 'Wait a moment,' he whispered back, and vanished into the parlour. Pretty soon the girls saw him making his way through the crowd with an immense slice of pound-cake in each hand.

'Here, Miss Rose,' he said, 'catch it.' But Rose ran half-way downstairs, received the cake, dimpled her thanks, and retreated to the darkness above, whence sounds proceeded which sent the amused Professor into the parlour convulsed with suppressed laughter. Pretty soon Clover stole up the backstairs to report.

'Are you having a nice time? Is the lemonade good? Who have you been talking with?' inquired a chorus of voices.

'Pretty nice. Everybody is very old. I haven't been talking to anybody in particular, and the lemonade is only cream-of-tartar water. I think it's jollier up here with you,' replied Clover. 'I must go now; my turn to play comes next.' Down she ran.

'Except for the glory of the thing, I think we're having more fun than she,' answered Rose.

Next week came St Valentine's Day. Several of the girls received valentines from home, and they wrote them to each other. Katy and Clover both had one from Phil, exactly alike, with the same purple bird in the middle of the page, and 'I love you' printed underneath; and they joined in fabricating a gorgeous one for Rose, which was supposed to come from Potemkin de Montmorency, the hero of the album. But the most surprising valentine was received by Miss Jane. It came with others, while all the household were at dinner. The girls saw her redden and look angry, but she put the letter in her pocket, and said nothing.

In the afternoon, it came out through Bella that 'Miss Jane's letter was in poetry, and that she was just as cross as possible about it.' Just before tea, Louisa came running down the Row, to No. 4, where Katy was sitting with Rose.

'Girls, what do you think? That letter which Miss Jane got this morning was a valentine, the most dreadful thing, but so funny!' she stopped to laugh.

'How do you know?' cried the other two.

'Miss Marsh told Alice Gibbons. She's a sort of cousin, you know; and Miss Marsh often tells her things. She says Miss Jane and Mrs Nipson are furious, and are determined to find out who sent it. It was from Mr Hardhack, Miss Jane's missionary – or no, not from Mr Hardhack, but from a cannibal who had just eaten Mr Hardhack up; and he sent Miss Jane a lock of his hair, and the recipe the tribe cooked him by. They found him 'very nice', he said, and 'He turned out quite tender.' That was one of the lines in the poem. Did you ever hear anything like it? Who do you suppose sent it?'

'Who could it have been?' cried the others. Katy had one moment's awful misgiving; but a glance at Rose's face, calm and innocent as a baby's, reassured her. It was impossible that she could have done this mischievous thing. Katy, you see, was not privy to that entry in Rose's journal, 'Pay Miss Jane off', nor aware that Rose had just written underneath, 'Did it. Feb. 14, 1869.'

Nobody ever found out the author of this audacious valentine. Rose kept her own counsel, and Miss Jane probably concluded that 'the better part of valour was discretion', for the threatened inquiries were never made.

And now it lacked but six weeks to the end of the term. The girls counted the days, and practised various devices to make them pass more quickly. Esther Dearborn, who had a turn for arithmetic, set herself to a careful calculation of how many hours, minutes, and seconds must pass before the happy time should come. Annie Silsbie strung forty-two tiny squares of cardboard on a thread, and each night slipped one off and burned it up in the candle. Others made diagrams of the time, with a division for each day, and every night scored off one with a sense of triumph. None of these devices made the time hasten. It never moved more slowly than now.

But though Katy's heart bounded at the thought of home till she could hardly bear the gladness, she owned to Clover, 'Do you know, much as I long to get away, I am half sorry to go! It is parting with something which we shall never have any more. Home is lovely, and I would rather be there than anywhere else; but if you and I live to be a hundred, we shall never be girls at boarding-school again.'

CHAPTER
13

PARADISE REGAINED

'Only seven days more to cross off,' said Clover, drawing her pencil through one of the squares on the diagram pinned beside her looking-glass, 'seven more, and then – oh, joy! – papa will be here, and we shall start for home.'

She was interrupted by the entrance of Katy, holding a letter, and looking pale and aggrieved.

'Oh, Clover,' she cried, 'just listen to this! Papa can't come for us. Isn't it too bad?' And she read:

Burnet, March 20th

MY DEAR GIRLS

I find that it will not be possible for me to come for you next week, as I intended. Several people are severely ill, and old Mrs Barlow struck down suddenly with paralysis, so I cannot leave. I am sorry, and so will you be; but there is no help for it. Fortunately, Mrs Hall has just heard that some friends of hers are coming west-ward with their family, and she has written to ask them to take charge of you. The drawback to this plan is, that you will have to travel alone as far as Albany, where Mr Peters (Mrs Hall's friend) will meet you. I have written to ask Mr Page to see you in the train, and under the care of the guard, on Tuesday morning. I hope you will get through without embarrassment. Mr Peters will be at the station in Albany to receive you; or, if anything should hinder him, you are to drive at once to the Delavan House, where they are staying. I enclose a cheque for your journey. If Dorry were five years older, I should send him after you.

The children are most impatient to have you back. Miss Finch has been suddenly called away by illness of her sister-in-law, so Elsie is keeping house till your return.

God bless you, my dear daughters, and send you safe.

Yours affectionately,

P. CARR

'Oh, dear!' said Clover, with her lip trembling, 'now papa won't see Rosy.'

'No,' said Katy, 'and Rosy and Louisa, and the rest won't see him. That is the worst of all. I wanted them to so much. And just think how dismal it will be to travel with people we don't know. It's too – too bad, I declare.'

'I do think old Mrs Barlow might have put off being ill just one week longer,' grumbled Clover. 'It takes away half the pleasure of going home.'

The girls might be excused for being cross, for this was a great disappointment. There was no help for it, however, as papa said. They could only sigh and submit. But the journey, to which they had looked forward so much, was no longer thought of as a pleasure, only a disagreeable necessity, something which must be endured in order that they might reach home.

Five, four, three days – the last little square was

crossed off, the last dinner was eaten, the last breakfast. There was much mourning over Katy and Clover among the girls who were to return for another year. Louisa and Ellen Gray were inconsolable; and Bella, with a very small pocket-handkerchief held tightly in her hand, clung to Katy every moment, crying, and declaring that she would not let her go. The last evening she followed her into No. 2 (where she was dreadfully in the way of packing), and after various odd contortions and mysterious half-spoken sentences, she said –

'Say, won't you tell if I tell you something?'

'What is it?' asked Katy, absently, as she folded and smoothed her best gown.

'Something,' repeated Bella, wagging her head mysteriously, and looking more like a thievish squirrel than ever.

'Well, what is it? Tell me.'

To Katy's surprise, Bella burst into a violent fit of crying.

'I'm very sorry I did it,' she sobbed – 'very sorry! And now you'll never love me any more.'

'Yes, I will. What is it? Do stop crying, Bella, dear, and tell me,' said Katy, alarmed at the violence of the sobs.

'It was for fun, really and truly it was. But I wanted some cake too,' protested Bella, sniffing very hard.

'What!'

'And I didn't think anybody would know. Berry Searles doesn't care a bit for us little girls, only for big ones. And I knew if I said "Bella" he'd never give me the cake. So I said "Miss Carr" instead.'

'Bella, did you write that note?' inquired Katy, almost too surprised to speak.

'Yes. And I tied a string to your blind, because I knew I could go in and draw it up when you were practising. But I didn't mean to do any harm; and when Mrs Florence was so cross, and changed your room, I was very sorry,' moaned Bella, digging her knuckles into her eyes. 'Won't you ever love me any more?' she demanded.

Katy lifted her into her lap, and talked so tenderly and seriously that her contrition, which was only half genuine, became real; and she cried in good earnest when Katy kissed her in token of forgiveness.

'Of course, you'll go at once to Mrs Nipson,' said Clover and Rose, when Katy imparted this surprising discovery.

'No, I think not. Why should I? It would only get poor little Bella into a dreadful scrape, and she's coming back again, you know. Mrs Nipson does not believe that story now – nobody does. We have "lived it down", just as I hoped we should. That is much better than having it contradicted.'

'I don't think so; and I should enjoy seeing that little wretch of a Bella well whipped,' persisted Rose.

But Katy was not to be shaken.

'To please me, promise that not a word shall be said about it,' she urged; and to please her the girls consented.

I think Katy was right in saying that Mrs Nipson no longer believed her guilty in the affair of the note. She had been very friendly to both the sisters of late; and when Clover carried in her album and asked for an autograph, she waxed quite sentimental and wrote, 'I would not exchange the modest Clover for the most brilliant flower in our beautiful parterre, so bring it back

I pray thee, to your affectionate teacher, Marianne Nipson'; which effusion quite overwhelmed 'the modest Clover', and called out the remark from Rose – 'Don't she wish she may get you!' Miss Jane said twice, 'I shall miss you, Katy,' a speech which, to quote Rose again, made Katy look as 'surprised as Balaam'. Rose herself was not coming back to school. She and the girls were half broken-hearted at parting. They lavished tears, kisses, promises of letters, and vows of eternal friendship. Neither of them, it was agreed, was ever to love anybody else so well. The final moment would have been almost too tragical, had it not been for a last bit of mischief on the part of Rose. It was after the stage was actually at the door, and she had her foot upon the step that, struck by a happy thought, she rushed upstairs again, collected the girls, and, each taking a window, they tore down the cotton, flung open sashes, and startled Mrs Nipson, who stood below, by the simultaneous waving therefrom of many white flags. Katy, who was already in the stage, had the full benefit of this performance. Always after that, when she thought of the Nunnery, her memory recalled this scene – Mrs Nipson in the doorway, Bella blubbering behind, and overhead the windows crowded with saucy girls, laughing and triumphantly flapping the long cotton strip which had for so many months obscured the daylight for them all.

At Springfield next morning she and Clover said good-bye to Mr Page and Lilly. The ride to Albany was easy and safe. With every mile their spirits rose. At last they were actually on the way home.

At Albany they looked anxiously about the crowded

depot for 'Mr Peters.' Nobody appeared at first, and they had time to grow nervous before they saw a gentle, careworn little man coming toward them in company with the conductor.

'I believe you are the young ladies I have come to meet,' he said. 'You must excuse my being late; I was detained by business. There is a great deal to do to move a family out West'; he wiped his forehead in a dispirited way. Then he put the girls into a carriage, and gave the driver a direction.

'We'd better leave your baggage at the office as we pass,' he said, 'because we have to get off so early in the morning.'

'How early?'

'The boat goes at six, but we ought to be on board by half-past five, so as to be well settled before she starts.'

'The boat?' said Katy, opening her eyes.

'Yes. Erie Canal, you know. Our furniture goes that way, so we judged it best to do the same, and keep an eye on it ourselves. Never be separated from your property, if you can help it, that's my maxim. It's the "Prairie Belle" – one of the finest boats on the Canal.'

'When do we get to Buffalo?' asked Katy, with an uneasy recollection of having heard that canal boats travel slowly.

'Buffalo? Let me see. This is Tuesday – Wednesday, Thursday – well, if we're lucky we ought to be there Friday evening; so, if we're not too late to catch the night boat on the lake, you'll reach home Saturday afternoon. Yes; I think we may pretty safely say Saturday afternoon.'

Four days! The girls looked at each other with dismay

too deep for words. Elsie was expecting them by Thursday at the latest. What should they do?

'Telegraph,' was the only answer that suggested itself. So Katy scribbled a despatch. 'Coming by canal. Don't expect us till Saturday,' which she begged Mr Peters to send; and she and Clover agreed in whispers that it was dreadful, but they must bear it as patiently as they could.

Oh, the patience which is needed on a canal! The motion which is not so much motion as standing still! The crazy impulse to jump out and help the crawling boat along by pushing it from behind! How one grows to hate the slow, monotonous glide, the dull banks, and to envy every swift-moving thing in sight, each man on horseback, each bird flying through the air.

Mrs Peters was a thin, anxious woman, who spent her life anticipating disasters of all sorts. She had her children with her, three little boys, and a teething baby, and such a load of bundles, and baskets, and brown-paper parcels, that Katy and Clover privately wondered how she could possibly have got through the journey without their help. Willy, the eldest boy, was always begging leave to go ashore and ride the towing horses; Sammy, the second, could only be kept quiet by means of crooked pins and fish-lines of blue yarn; while Paul, the youngest, was possessed with a curiosity as to the under side of the boat, which resulted in his dropping his new hat overboard five times in three days, Mr Peters and the cabin-boy rowing back in a small boat each time to recover it. Mrs Peters sat on the deck with her baby in her lap, and was in perpetual agony lest the locks should work wrongly, or the boys be drowned, or some one fail to notice the warning cry, 'Bridge!' and have their heads carried off from their shoulders. Nobody did; but the poor lady suffered the anguish of ten accidents in dreading the one which never took place. The berths at night were small and cramped, restless children woke and cried, the cabins were close, the decks cold and windy. There was nothing to see, and nothing to do. Katy and Clover agreed that they never wanted to see a canal-boat again.

They were very helpful to Mrs Peters, amused the boys, and kept them out of mischief; and she told her husband that she really thought she shouldn't have lived through the journey if it hadn't been for the Miss Carrs, they were such kind girls, and so fond of children. But the three days were terribly long. At last they ended. Buffalo was reached in time for the lake boat; and once established on board, feeling the rapid motion, and knowing that each stroke of the paddles took them nearer home, the girls were rewarded for their long trial of patience.

At four o'clock the next afternoon Burnet was in sight. Long before they touched the wharf Clover discovered old Whitey and the carriage, and Alexander, waiting for them among the crowds of carriages. Standing on the edge of the dock appeared a well-known figure.

'Papa! Papa!' she shrieked. It seemed as if the girls could not wait for the boat to stop, and the plank to be lowered. How delightful it was to feel papa again! Such a sense of home and comfort and shelter as came with his touch!

'I'll never go away from you again, never, never!' repeated Clover, keeping tight hold of his hand as they drove up the hill. Dr Carr, as he gazed at his girls, was equally happy – they were so bright, so affectionate, and loving. No, he could never spare them again, for boarding-school or anything else, he thought.

'You must be very tired,' he said.

'Not a bit. I'm hardly ever tired now,' replied Katy.

'Oh, dear! I forgot to thank Mr Peters for taking care of us,' said Clover.

'Never mind. I did it for you,' answered her father.

'Oh, that baby!' she continued; 'how glad I am that it has gone to Toledo, and I needn't hear it cry any more! Katy! Katy! there's home! We are at the gate!'

The girls looked eagerly out, but no children were visible. They hurried up the gravel path, under the locust boughs just beginning to bud. There, over the front door, was an arch of evergreens, with 'Katy' and 'Clover' upon it in scarlet letters; and as they reached the porch, the door flew open, and out poured the children in a tumultuous little crowd. They had been on the roof, looking through a spy-glass after the boat.

'We never knew you had come till we heard the gate,' explained John and Dorry; while Elsie hugged Clover, and Phil, locking his arms round Katy's neck, took his feet off the floor, and swung them in an ecstasy of affection, until she begged for mercy.

'How you are grown! Dorry, you're as tall as I am! Elsie, darling, how well you look. Oh, isn't it delicious, delicious, delicious, to be at home again!' There was such a hubbub of endearments and explanations, that Dr Carr could hardly make himself heard.

'Clover, your waist has grown as small as a pin. You look just like the beautiful princess in Elsie's story,' said Johnnie.

'Take the girls into the parlour,' repeated Dr Carr.

'Take 'em upstairs! You don't know what is upstairs!' shouted Phil, whereupon Elsie frowned and shook her head at him.

The parlour was gay with daffodils and hyacinths and vases of blue violets, which smelt delightfully. Cecy had helped to arrange them, Elsie said. And just at that moment Cecy herself came in. Her hair was arranged in a sort of pincushion of puffs, with a row of curls on top, where no curls used to grow, and her appearance generally was very fine and fashionable; but she was the same affectionate Cecy as ever, and hugged the girls, and danced round them as she used to do at twelve. She had waited until they had had time to kiss once all round, she said, and then she really couldn't wait any longer.

'Now, come upstairs,' suggested Elsie, when Clover had warmed her feet, and the flowers had been admired, and everybody had said ten times over how nice it was to have the girls back, and the girls had replied that it was just as nice to come back.

So they all went upstairs, Elsie leading the way.

'Where are you going?' cried Katy; 'that's the blue-room.' But Elsie did not pause.

'You see,' she explained, with the door-knob in her hand, 'papa and I thought you ought to have a bigger room now, because you are grown-up young ladies! So we have fixed this for you, and your old one is going to be the spare room instead.' Then she threw the door open, and led the girls in.

'See, Katy,' she said, 'this is your bureau, and this is Clover's. And see what nice drawers papa has had put in the closet – two for you, and two for her. Aren't they convenient? Don't you like it? And isn't it a great deal pleasanter than the old room?'

'Oh, a great deal!' cried the girls. 'It is delightful, everything about it.' All Katy's old treasures had been transferred from her old quarters to this. There was her cushioned chair, her table, her book-shelf, the pictures from the walls. There were some new things too – a blue carpet, fresh paper on the walls, window curtains of fresh chintz; and Elsie had made a tasteful pincushion for each bureau, and Johnnie crocheted mats for the wash-stand. Altogether, it was as pretty a bower as two sisters just grown into young ladies could desire.

'What are those lovely things hanging on either side of the bed?' asked Clover.

They were two illuminated texts, sent as a 'welcome home', by Cousin Helen. One was a morning text, and the other an evening text, Elsie explained. The evening text, which bore the words, 'I will lay me down to sleep, and take my rest, for it is Thou, Lord, only Who makest me dwell in safety,' was painted in soft purples and greys, and among the poppies and silver lilies which wreathed it appeared a cunning little downy bird, fast asleep, with his head under his wing. The morning text, 'When I awake, I am still with Thee,' was in bright colours, scarlet and blue and gold, and had a frame of rose garlands and wide-awake-looking butterflies and humming-birds. The girls thought they had never seen anything so pretty.

Such a gay supper as they had that night! Katy would not take her old place at the tea-tray. She wanted to know how Elsie looked as housekeeper, she said.

'I'll begin tomorrow,' said Katy.

And with that morrow, when she came out of her pretty room and took her place once more as manager of the household, her grown-up life may be said to have begun. So it is time that I should cease to write about her. Grown-up lives may be very interesting, but they have no rightful place in a child's book. If little girls will forget to be little, and take it upon them to become young ladies, they must bear the consequences, one of which is, that we can follow their fortunes no longer.

I wrote these last words sitting in the same green meadow where the first words of 'What Katy Did' were written. A year had passed, but a cardinal-flower which seemed the same stood looking at itself in the brook, and from the bulrush-bed sounded tiny voices. My little goggle-eyed friends were discussing Katy and her conduct, as they did then, but with less spirit; for one voice came seldom and faintly, while the other, bold and defiant as ever, repeated over and over again, 'Katy didn't! Katy didn't! She didn't, didn't, didn't.'

'Katy did!' sounded faintly from the farther rush.

'She didn't, she didn't,' chirped the undaunted partisan.

'Katy didn't.' The words repeated themselves in my mind, as I walked homeward. How much room for 'Didn'ts' is in the world, I thought. What an important part they play. And how glad I am that, with all her own and other people's doings, so many of these very 'Didn'ts' were included among the things which my Katy did at school!